THE
HOME
BARTENDER
SECOND EDITION

Over 175 Drinks with Four Ingredients or Less

SHANE CARLEY

Author of *The Mason Jar Cocktail Companion*

CIDER MILL
PRESS

BOOK
PUBLISHERS
KENNEBUNKPORT, MAINE

In memory of Betty,
loved and missed by all.

THE HOME BARTENDER, SECOND EDITION

13-Digit ISBN: 978-1604338126
10-Digit ISBN: 1604338121

This book may be ordered by mail from the publisher. Please include $5.99 for postage and handling. Please support your local bookseller first!

Books published by Cider Mill Press Book Publishers are available at special discounts for bulk purchases in the United States by corporations, institutions, and other organizations. For more information, please contact the publisher.

Cider Mill Press Book Publishers
"Where good books are ready for press"
12 Spring Street, PO Box 454
Kennebunkport, Maine 04046

Visit us online! www.cidermillpress.com

Image Credits: Photos by Appleseed Press Book Publishers: Cover, and pages 1, 2, 3, 18, 19, 86, 87, 114, 118, 120, 140, 148, 149, 152, 153, 164, 170, 171, 180, 188, 190, 210, 211, 226, 228, 238, 242, 243, 292, 310, 314, 320, 322, 323, 350, 358, 362, 364, and 368.

All other images used under official license from Shutterstock.com.

Glassware icons by Shutterstock; all ingredient icons by Shutterstock or Appleseed Press Book Publishers.

Printed in China

11 12 13 14

Second Edition

CONTENTS

INTRODUCTION 5

BUILDING YOUR HOME BAR 6

VODKA 11

RUM 78

GIN 141

INTRODUCTION

Cocktails can be complicated. With so many drinks featuring what feels like dozens of ingredients, being mixed together in increasingly complicated and diverse ways, it isn't hard to feel out of your depth when it comes to mixology.

But it doesn't have to be that way! Some of the best cocktails in the world feature only a couple of ingredients, shaken or stirred together in simple proportions, and ready to drink in seconds. Everyone knows that sometimes simplicity is the way to go—not just for the sake of convenience but for taste as well. After all, who needs eight different ingredients muddling their flavors together when all you really want is something to accent the great taste of your whiskey or rum?

You'll see the terms Classic, Perfect, and Budget being thrown around in this book. Their meanings are simple: the Classic version of a drink is a by-the-book version that you can't go wrong with. The Perfect version is a drink made with only the best ingredients. And the Budget version is a simpler, more affordable cocktail that will still taste great.

The Home Bartender features the best of the best when it comes to simple cocktails. With classic cocktails you'll recognize and new drinks you're sure to love, there's something for everyone here. Whether you're looking for some new vodka drinks or looking to bust out an old tequila recipe, *The Home Bartender* is the perfect book for any home bar!

BUILDING YOUR HOME BAR

When it comes to mixology, you should never feel like you have to spend hundreds of dollars on obscure liqueurs just to mix a cocktail you might drink once a month. As long as you have the basics covered, you should feel pretty good! The truth is, while some exotic cocktails might call for specialty ingredients like Chambord or crème de cassis, you'd be surprised how many perfectly delicious drinks can be made with good old-fashioned whiskey, gin, vodka, tequila, and rum.

That said, there are ingredients that are more common than others, and adding a few flavorful liqueurs to your home bar will give you options you might never have considered. From coconut rum to orange liqueur, these are the basics that can help you build a home bar that will impress your guests, with options ranging from bargain bin must-haves to top-shelf favorites.

BASIC BOTTLES

Vodka
Budget: Svedka
Classic: Skyy
Perfect: Grey Goose

Gin
Budget: Seagram's
Classic: Tanqueray
Perfect: Bombay Sapphire

Rum
Budget: Bacardi
Classic: Captain Morgan
Perfect: El Dorado

Tequila
Budget: Agavales
Classic: Jose Cuervo
Perfect: 1800

Whiskey
Budget: Evan Williams
Classic: Maker's Mark
Perfect: Woodford Reserve

Must-Have Mixers
Triple Sec
Sweet Vermouth
Lime Juice
Lemon Juice
Bitters
Grenadine
Simple Syrup

Nice to Have
Dry Vermouth
Kahlua
Crème de Menthe
Malibu Coconut Rum
Blue Curacao

Wish List
Campari
Orgeat Syrup
Flavored Bitters

BAR TOOLS

Sometimes mixing a drink is as simple as pouring the ingredients. Other times, you need to do a little more. Bar tools are there to make your life a bit easier when it comes to mixing up these more complicated cocktails. From the cocktail shaker to the muddler, these are the tools that you should be sure to have in your home bar.

Must-Haves

Cocktail Shaker
Strainer
Jigger
Knife
Bottle Opener
Corkscrew

Nice to Have

Cocktail Stirrer
Muddler
Juicer
Zester

GLASSWARE

Must-Haves

Pint Glass
Shot Glass
Old Fashioned Glass
Highball Glass

Nice to Have

Margarita Glass
Cocktail Glass
Champagne Flute
Mason Jar

Wish List

Hurricane Glass
Daiquiri Glass
Irish Coffee Glass
Sour Glass

PARTY MIXERS

If you're having a party, you'll want to have a few of these on hand for easy mixing! Even if you aren't looking to mix up specific cocktails, these mixers go great with most types of alcohol and will keep a majority of party guests happy.

Coca-Cola	Tonic Water	Maraschino Cherries
Sprite	Club Soda	Oranges
Ginger Ale	Ice	Mint
Cranberry Juice	Lemons	
Fruit Punch	Limes	

VODKA

If there's one type of liquor that people tend to have lying around the house, it's vodka. And why not? Vodka's taste isn't particularly assertive, and it can take on the flavor of just about anything, contributing a healthy bite of alcohol into otherwise unexciting drinks.

The idea behind *The Home Bartender* is that cocktails don't have to be complicated. They don't have to have 100 different flavors vying for the attention of your palate. In fact, most cocktails don't call for more than four ingredients. And sometimes the very best cocktails are those thrown together with whatever you happened to have lying around. So, what better spirit to lead off with than vodka?

In the following pages, you'll find recipes both old and new, familiar and unfamiliar, with a new spin on some classic tastes, and a variety of different ways to inject a little boozy goodness into a simple mix of flavors. Vodka cocktails are simple, fresh, and, above all, adaptable. You're sure to find something you like, so give it a try!

LONG ISLAND EXPRESS

The Long Island Iced Tea is one of the most popular (and strong) cocktails on planet Earth, but it has far more than four ingredients (in fact, it has more than four different *liquors* alone). Still, the spirit of the cocktail should live on, and it does just that in the Long Island Express. Trimming some of the fat (not *literal* fat—that would be disgusting) from the original recipe, we are left with a simple vodka-and-cola recipe, with a few extra ingredients to ensure that you won't want for flavor.

BASIC INGREDIENTS

 1/2 lemon (juiced)

 1 part vodka

 1 splash triple sec

 2 parts cola

 1 lemon slice (garnish)

GLASSWARE:
Highball glass.

1. Juice the lemon over ice, then add the vodka and a splash of triple sec.

2. Add cola to fill, then stir until thoroughly mixed.

3. Garnish with a slice of lemon.

VARIATION. The Long Island Iced Tea traditionally contains vodka, rum, tequila, and gin. If you think it sounds better to make the Long Island Express with any of the other liquors rather than vodka, the flavors should hold up well regardless of which liquor you choose to use as a base.

NON ISLAND ICED TEA

While the traditional Long Island Iced Tea is built around many different types of alcohol, the Non Island Iced Tea is a combination of different refreshing beverages. On their own, iced tea, lemonade, and cola are delicious. Together, they make something a little bit more....unusual? Sure. But why not go out on a limb once in a while?

BASIC INGREDIENTS

 I part iced tea (unsweetened)

 I part lemonade

 I part cola

 I lemon slice (garnish)

 GLASSWARE: Highball glass.

1. Add the ingredients together in your glass. Stir until mixed.

2. Garnish with a lemon slice.

CAPESCREW

Two of the most famous vodka cocktails are the Screwdriver, traditionally consisting of vodka and orange juice, and the Cape Cod, made with vodka and cranberry juice. Well, as any seasoned breakfaster will surely tell you, few flavors go together quite as well as orange juice and cranberry juice. Mixed together, they create a flavor combination of sweet and tart that can tantalize any palate. Add in a little vodka and triple sec, and you've got the Capescrew, a combination of two favorites that takes both to the next level.

BASIC INGREDIENTS

 I part vodka

 I splash triple sec

 I part orange juice

 I part cranberry juice

 I orange wheel (garnish)

 GLASSWARE:
Highball glass.

1. Pour the vodka over ice and add a splash of triple sec.

2. Add the orange juice and cranberry juice and stir until thoroughly mixed.

3. Garnish with an orange wheel.

VARIATIONS

- For more fruity flavor, try orange vodka or cranberry vodka instead of unflavored vodka. Or play with the ratios to get just the right flavor.
- The Capescrew is similar to the Sex on the Beach, which features slightly different ratios and peach schnapps in place of triple sec. Give that one a whirl!

SEA BREEZE

A traditional vodka cocktail, the Sea Breeze plays with a variety of citrus flavors to create a sweet concoction perfect for relaxing on the beach on a hot summer day. Grapefruit, cranberry, and lime juice bounce off one another as the drink reaches your tongue, providing a cool, crisp, and refreshing counterbalance to the sun beating down on you.

BASIC INGREDIENTS

 1/2 lime (juiced)

 1 part vodka

 2 parts cranberry juice

 1 part grapefruit juice

 1 lime wedge (garnish)

 Cherry (garnish)

 GLASSWARE:
Highball glass.

1. Juice half a lime over ice, then add vodka.

2. Add cranberry juice and grapefruit juice and stir until thoroughly mixed.

3. Garnish with a lime wedge and a cherry.

DON'T HAVE FRESH LEMONS OR LIMES?

Don't fret! You can always use lemon or lime juice from the store. The average lemon contains about 3 tablespoons of juice, while the average lime contains about 2 tablespoons. If your drink calls for the juice of ½ lime, you can easily deduce that they're asking for 1 tablespoon of lime juice.

BLASTOFF

Vodka cocktails are great, but sometimes you don't need an entire glass to get the job done. Shots can be a tricky thing, but when they're good, they're very good. It takes a certain amount of skill to impart enough flavor into that one gulp to make you say "that was great!" Such is the case with the Blastoff cocktail, one swallow of which will pucker your mouth and electrify your palate.

BASIC INGREDIENTS

1 oz. vodka

1/2 oz. grapefruit juice

1 squeeze lemon juice

1 squeeze lime juice

GLASSWARE:
Shot glass.

1. Pour the vodka and grapefruit juice into a shot glass and finish with a quick squeeze of lemon and lime juice.

BORROWED THYME

Borrowed Thyme is similar to the Blastoff cocktail (page 18), but it abandons the lemon and lime elements in favor of more herbal notes. If you've ever had thyme-infused lemonade, you know that it's an herb that works very well with citrus. Borrowed Thyme capitalizes on that, mixing thyme and grapefruit to create a taste that is sure to delight.

BASIC INGREDIENTS:

 I part vodka

 I part club soda

 3 parts grapefruit juice

 4 sprigs thyme

GLASSWARE:
 Old Fashioned glass.

1. Add the vodka, club soda, grapefruit juice, and 3 sprigs of thyme to a pint glass filled with ice.

2. Stir until thoroughly mixed.

3. Strain the resulting mixture into an Old Fashioned glass filled with ice.

4. Garnish with the remaining sprig of thyme.

WHITE RUSSIAN

What could be better than a White Russian? This simple mixture of vodka, coffee liqueur, and cream provides a rich, delicious, and refreshing flavor perfect for summer and winter alike!

BASIC INGREDIENTS

 I part vodka

 I part coffee liqueur

 2 parts cream

 GLASSWARE:
Old Fashioned glass.

1. Fill an Old Fashioned glass with ice and add the vodka and coffee liqueur.

2. Slowly pour the cream over the vodka mixture.

3. Stir the ingredients together slowly.

Some prefer to keep the cream and the liquor as separated as possible, even when drinking. This is up to the preference of the drinker, but you may find that the bottom of the drink is difficult to drink without the addition of cream. By mixing them together, you'll get a nice, rich, golden beverage in your glass.

THE DIRTY SPY

The vodka martini is, of course, the drink that James Bond made famous, though it was already one of the most popular drinks in the world when 007 put in his first order. Martini drinkers will know that the famous spy's request for his cocktail to be "shaken, not stirred" was an unusual one, as the martini is not typically prepared this way. In honor of this unusual request, The Dirty Spy is a simple dirty martini prepared in a cocktail shaker.

BASIC INGREDIENTS

3 parts vodka

I part dry vermouth

I splash green olive brine

I pimento-stuffed green olive

GLASSWARE:
Cocktail glass.

1. Add the vodka, vermouth, and olive brine to a cocktail shaker filled with ice. Shake well.

2. Strain the resulting mixture into a cocktail glass and add the olive (or a couple).

VARIATIONS

- While The Dirty Spy makes use of olives and olive brine, a traditional martini simply uses a lemon twist as a garnish.
- The original martini was made with gin, so if you find the taste of juniper more to your liking, you can always try that!

CREAMSICLE

If you're like me, you grew up eating Creamsicle popsicles, and this drink captures that flavor. This delicious combination of orange and cream will sweep you straight back to your childhood on a wave of nostalgia—with an adult twist.

BASIC INGREDIENTS

 I part orange juice

 I part vodka

 I part cream

 I splash triple sec

 I orange slice (garnish)

 GLASSWARE:
Old Fashioned glass.

1. Stir the ingredients together in a mixing glass.

2. Strain the resulting mixture into an Old Fashioned Glass filled with ice.

3. Garnish with an orange slice.

VARIATION

As always, the ratios can be adjusted until you find a drink that you suits you. Mixology may have become an increasingly popular skill, but it's far from an exact science. The purpose of every cocktail is for the drinker to enjoy it, and that should always be your end goal.

STRAWBERRIES AND CREAM

The Creamsicle is a delicious drink, but the orange isn't the only fruit known to pair well with cream. Enter the Strawberries and Cream cocktail, combining vanilla and strawberry vodka with some rich cream to create a tasty, filling, and—thanks to the grenadine—colorful cocktail.

BASIC INGREDIENTS

1 part strawberry vodka

1 part vanilla vodka

2 parts cream

1 splash grenadine

1 fresh strawberry (garnish)

GLASSWARE:
Old Fashioned glass.

1. Pour the strawberry vodka and vanilla vodka over ice. Top with cream and stir until thoroughly mixed.

2. Finish with a splash of grenadine for color. Garnish with a fresh strawberry.

WHAT'S THE DIFFERENCE BETWEEN A DASH AND A SPLASH?

They're definitely inexact measurements, but a dash is a tiny addition, just enough to impart a little flavor. A splash is a bit bigger—essentially a quick pour into the drink. If you feel the need for an exact measurement, you can use a teaspoon for a dash and a tablespoon for a splash.

MINT MULE

6 mint leaves

1 lime wedge (juiced)

1 part vodka

2 parts ginger beer

1 lime wheel (garnish)

Turn the page for the recipe!

⟶

MINT MULE

The Moscow Mule is a popular vodka cocktail featuring primarily vodka and ginger beer. The sharpness of each of those flavors make this a winning combination, but sometimes it can be a bit much. The Moscow Mule is typically tempered with a bit of lime juice, but let's further take it down by adding a bit of mint to the party as well.

BASIC INGREDIENTS

 6 mint leaves

 1 lime wedge (juiced)

 1 part vodka

 2 parts ginger beer

 1 lime wheel (garnish)

 GLASSWARE:
Highball glass
(or copper mug).

1. Tear the mint leaves in half to release the flavor, then add them to the bottom of the glass.

2. Add the juice from the lime wedge and muddle the mint leaves. Add ice.

3. Pour in the vodka and ginger beer. Stir until thoroughly mixed.

4. Garnish with a lime wheel.

HOW DO YOU MUDDLE INGREDIENTS? It's easy. Simply put them at the bottom of your glass and use a blunt instrument to lightly mash them together. You can use a muddler, but if you don't have one, the back of a spoon will work just fine.

VIRGIN MULE

The Virgin Mule is a delicious and refreshing alternative to its boozy namesake, and you can drink as many of them as you please!

BASIC INGREDIENTS

 1/2 lime (juiced)

 8 oz. ginger beer

 1 lime slice (garnish)

 GLASSWARE:
Highball glass
(or copper mug).

1. Juice the lime into your glass, then add ice.

2. Add ginger beer to fill, then garnish with a slice of lime.

RING #4

You know what's better than three? Four. The Ring #4 combines a splash of four different fruit flavors into an inviting mix sure to make you feel like a champion. The grenadine adds a gorgeous red color that makes this drink feel like a throwback to summer days spent sitting on the porch with a refreshing glass of raspberry lemonade. Whether you're downing these in August or February, the tasty combination of fruit flavors is sure to have you coming back for two, three, or even 12.

BASIC INGREDIENTS

 1 part raspberry vodka

 1 splash triple sec

 2 parts lemonade

 1 splash grenadine

 1 lemon wheel (garnish)

 GLASSWARE:
Highball glass.

1. Add ice to a highball glass and then add the vodka and triple sec.

2. Fill the rest of the glass with lemonade and top with a splash of grenadine to add an inviting red hue to the drink.

3. Garnish with a lemon wheel.

If there are four things that every home bar should have (outside of the standard categories of alcohol), they are vermouth (sweet and dry), bitters, grenadine, and triple sec. These ingredients are called for in small amounts in hundreds of cocktails, and can be used to spice up a wide variety of drinks.

RING #5

Ring #4 is good, but Ring #5 is unequivocally the sweetest. This is a delicious brunch cocktail that captures the feel of sangria without all the hassle. The simple addition of a handful of blueberries and raspberries gives this drink a festive red, white, and blue look when served over ice, and the fresh fruit will help you stage a comeback from even the roughest night. Let this tasty treat return you to MVP form!

BASIC INGREDIENTS:

1 part raspberry vodka

2 parts club soda

1 splash grenadine

Blueberries (garnish)

Raspberries (garnish)

GLASSWARE:
Highball glass.

1. Add a handful of blueberries and raspberries to a highball glass, then fill the glass with ice.

2. Add raspberry vodka and club soda.

3. Top with a splash (or more) of grenadine until drink achieves desired color.

CLASSIC
COSMOPOLITAN

2 parts Skyy Vodka

1 part triple sec

1 part cranberry juice

1 splash lime juice

1 lime wheel (garnish)

Turn the page for the recipe!

→

CLASSIC COSMOPOLITAN

Known for being fruity, delicious, and, well, *pink*, the cosmopolitan is one of the tastiest and most popular vodka drinks around. Oddly, men tend to shy away from ordering the cosmopolitan. It's a shame, really. It's the same color as a Cape Cod or a greyhound, and it's served in more or less the same way as a martini. Regardless, the cosmopolitan is a delicious, sweet, and fruity drink perfect for a night out on the town or a cozy night in the apartment.

BASIC INGREDIENTS

2 parts Skyy Vodka

1 part triple sec

1 part cranberry juice

1 splash lime juice

1 lime wheel (garnish)

GLASSWARE:
Cocktail glass.

1. Fill a cocktail shaker with ice and add the liquid ingredients. Shake well.

2. Strain the resulting mixture into a cocktail glass and garnish with a lime wheel.

PERFECT COSMOPOLITAN

If you're drinking a classic cocktail like the cosmopolitan, why not go all the way with it? Use only the finest ingredients and you might be surprised to discover that this already delicious treat can actually get even tastier. Make sure you're using the freshest ingredients, too—that means fresh squeezed limes only!

BASIC INGREDIENTS

 2 parts Grey Goose Vodka

 1 part triple sec

 1 part cranberry juice

 1 lime wedge (juiced)

 1 lime wheel (garnish)

 **GLASSWARE:** Cocktail glass.

1. Fill a cocktail shaker with ice and add the vodka, triple sec, cranberry juice, and lime juice (squeeze the lime straight in). Shake well.

2. Strain the resulting mixture into a cocktail glass and garnish with a lime wheel.

BUDGET COSMOPOLITAN

Then again, why go over the top for a cocktail that's really little more than a mixture of three different fruit flavors, with a splash of vodka thrown in for good measure? If that's your mentality, then maybe the Budget Cosmo is for you. Never mind the garnishes and who needs fresh limes? Grab the vodka you've got on the shelf, mix it up until it's nice and pink, and presto! Deliciousness.

BASIC INGREDIENTS

2 parts Svedka Vodka

1 part triple sec

1 part cranberry juice

1 splash lime juice

GLASSWARE:
Cocktail glass.

1. Fill a cocktail shaker with ice and add the vodka, triple sec, cranberry juice, and lime juice. Shake well.

2. Strain the resulting mixture into a cocktail glass and garnish with a lime wheel.

VIRGIN COSMOPOLITAN

Forget the booze and rock out this summer with the Virgin Cosmopolitan, a classy and colorful way to keep cool while remaining sober. The Virgin Cosmopolitan combines the delicious flavors that you'll find in any standard cosmopolitan and gives them a splash of fizz while passing on the vodka. It's a surprisingly good way to spice up a sober evening, and it's the perfect drink for any designated driver.

BASIC INGREDIENTS

 4 parts cranberry juice

 1 lime wedge (juiced)

 1 splash Sprite

 1 lime wheel (garnish)

 **GLASSWARE:**
Cocktail glass.

1. Add the cranberry juice to a cocktail glass and squeeze in the juice from the lime wedge.

2. Top with a splash of Sprite.

3. Garnish with a lime wheel.

BETTY'S COSMO

If you love cosmos and want to try something a little bit different, give Betty's Cosmo a try. With equal parts vodka and cranberry juice cocktail, and a tantalizing mixture of fresh lime juice and its sweetened counterpart, Betty's Cosmo is a delicious drink perfect for serving at family gatherings or sipping on the back porch.

BASIC INGREDIENTS

3 oz. Skyy vodka

3 oz. cranberry juice cocktail

1 oz. Cointreau

1 dash Rose's Lime Juice

1 squeeze fresh lime juice

GLASSWARE:
Cocktail glass.

1. Add the vodka, cranberry juice cocktail, Cointreau, and Rose's Lime Juice to a cocktail shaker filled with ice. Shake well.

2. Strain the resulting mixture into a cocktail glass.

3. Top with a squeeze of fresh lime juice.

SUMMER SPLASH

Cosmopolitans are nice, but maybe you want something a little different. A little less...pink? The Summer Splash takes a few of the best elements of the cosmopolitan and combines them into a light, refreshing flavored lemonade. It's a citrusy take on a classic cocktail, and one that you (and the guests at your summer cookout) are sure to love.

BASIC INGREDIENTS:

 1 part cranberry vodka

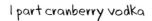 2 parts lemonade

 1 splash lime juice

GLASSWARE:
Cocktail glass.

1. Fill a cocktail shaker with ice and add the vodka, lemonade, and lime juice. Shake well.

2. Strain the resulting mixture into a cocktail glass.

BLUE FIREFLIES

Blue Fireflies is a delicious cocktail that changes as you drink it. The primary flavors at play here are vodka, lemon, and lime, but as the Blue Curaçao ice cubes melt, the drink takes on a blue hue and a bit of orange flavor begins to seep in. This gives the cocktail an alluring, transformative quality.

BASIC INGREDIENTS:

 1 part vodka

 2 parts Sprite

 1 splash fresh lime juice

 3 Blue Curaçao ice cubes

 GLASSWARE:
Highball glass.

1. Make ice cubes using Blue Curaçao.

2. Add three Blue Curaçao ice cubes to a highball glass.

3. Add vodka, Sprite, and fresh lime juice.

4. Stir together.

> Making ice cubes with Blue Curaçao is simple. Although alcohol does not freeze at 0°C, the alcohol content of Blue Curaçao is low enough to freeze in a regular home freezer. Simply fill an ice cube tray with Blue Curaçao and let it sit in the freezer for a few hours. The ice cubes will melt quickly and have a slightly slushy quality to them, adding a textural element to the drink as well.

PEACH TREE ICED TEA

What's better than a little peach iced tea on a summer day? Iced tea is one of the most refreshing drinks on the planet, so adding a little vodka to the mix can't go awry. And where better to get that peach flavor that makes you feel all warm and fuzzy than by adding a little peach schnapps? Peach Tree Iced Tea is a drink that towers over other iced tea cocktails. Is it the best one out there? You be the judge.

BASIC INGREDIENTS

6 mint leaves

1 part peach schnapps

1 part vodka

2 parts iced tea

GLASSWARE:
Highball glass.

1. Tear the mint leaves in half and add them to the bottom of your glass. Add the peach schnapps and muddle together.

2. Add ice to the glass, then pour in the vodka and iced tea. Stir until thoroughly mixed.

LIQUID
APPLE PIE

1 part vanilla vodka

1 dash brown sugar

3 parts apple cider

1 dash cinnamon

1 cinnamon stick (garnish)

Turn the page for the recipe!

LIQUID APPLE PIE

This drink captures what you love most about the flavor of homemade apple pie and puts it in a glass instead of on a plate. In fact, the drink tastes so good that you might not even realize how many you've had. Much like when eating mom's apple pie, moderation is key!

BASIC INGREDIENTS

 I part vanilla vodka

 I dash brown sugar

 3 parts apple cider

 I dash cinnamon

 I cinnamon stick (garnish)

 GLASSWARE:
Mason jar
or glass mug.

1. Add the vanilla vodka and brown sugar to your glass and stir them together.

2. Pour the apple cider over top and finish with a dusting of cinnamon.

3. Garnish with a cinnamon stick.

VARIATIONS

- While you can drink it cold, the drink is (in my humble opinion) considerably better when served warm.
- If you're feeling particularly festive, garnish with a star anise.

VIRGIN APPLE PIE

Virgin Apple Pie is another liquid way to evoke memories of crisp, cool, fall evenings—but without worrying about a hangover in the morning.

BASIC INGREDIENTS

 3 parts apple cider

 1 part cream soda

 1 dash cinnamon

 1 dollop whipped cream (garnish)

 GLASSWARE:
Glass mug.

1. Add the apple cider and cream soda to your glass.

2. Top with a dash of cinnamon, then stir until thoroughly mixed.

3. Add a dollop of whipped cream if you wish.

CHERRY LIME SPIKE

Cherry and lime have traditionally gone well together, but rather than drink a regular old glass of cherry limeade, why not spike it with a little vodka? A little cherry vodka can go a long way, both in terms of adding alcohol to the cocktail and adding flavor.

BASIC INGREDIENTS

 I part cherry vodka

 I part lime juice

 2 parts club soda

 I dash grenadine

I lime wheel (garnish)

GLASSWARE:
Highball glass.

1. Pour the cherry vodka and lime juice into your glass and stir together. Add ice.

2. Add club soda to fill, then top with a small dash of grenadine for color.

3. Garnish with a lime wheel.

VARIATION

Use limeade or lime-flavored club soda instead of lime juice.

THE ESSENTIAL BLOODY MARY

1 dash Worcestershire sauce

1 dash lemon juice

1 part vodka

2 parts tomato juice

Garnish with anything your heart desires

Turn the page for the recipe!

⟶

THE ESSENTIAL BLOODY MARY

The Essential Bloody Mary takes the Bloody Mary and distills (no pun intended) it down to its most essential ingredients for your mixing pleasure.

BASIC INGREDIENTS

 I dash Worcestershire sauce

 I dash lemon juice

 I part vodka

 2 parts tomato juice

 Garnish with anything your heart desires

 GLASSWARE: Pint glass.

1. Add the Worcestershire sauce and lemon juice to a pint glass, then add ice.

2. Pour in the vodka and tomato juice and stir until thoroughly mixed.

3. Garnish with bacon, olives, lemon wedges, celery, pickles, an entire hamburger, or anything else your heart desires.

The Bloody Mary is a simple drink, but it's been complicated by the expectation of increasingly outrageous garnishes. From a simple rasher of bacon to an entire bacon cheeseburger, the garnishes for this traditional drink have gotten out of control. This isn't a bad thing—now you can add whatever you like to your Bloody Mary without fear of getting strange looks from anyone!

VIRGIN MARY

A Bloody Mary is tasty, but then so is regular old tomato juice. Spice up your tomato juice with a few of the fixings that the Bloody Mary is famous for, giving you a great new drink with which to greet the day!

BASIC INGREDIENTS

 8 oz. tomato juice

 1 dash Worcestershire sauce

 1 dash lemon juice

 1 dash pepper

 Garnish with anything your heart desires

 GLASSWARE: Pint glass.

1. Add ice to your glass, then fill with tomato juice.

2. Add a dash of Worcestershire sauce, lemon juice, and black pepper. Stir thoroughly.

3. Garnish with anything you please.

VARIATION

This is just the base for a successful Virgin Mary. If you'd like to add other common ingredients (like horseradish or salt, for example) that you happen to have lying around, you can easily build off this recipe.

VODKA SUNRISE

As beautiful as it is traditional, the Vodka Sunrise is a drink popular both for its tasty flavor and gorgeous hues. Its appearance lives up to its name—the cocktail looks like nothing so much as the sun rising over the horizon in the morning, with reds, oranges, and yellows playing off one another in a fantastic medley of color.

BASIC INGREDIENTS

1 part vodka

1 dash lemon juice

2 parts orange juice

1 splash grenadine

1 maraschino cherry (garnish)

1 orange slice (garnish)

GLASSWARE:
Highball glass.

1. Add ice to a glass and pour in the vodka and lemon juice. Mix together.

2. Add orange juice to fill, then top with a splash of grenadine. Rather than stirring, allow the grenadine to slowly filter down through the orange juice and vodka.

3. Garnish with a maraschino cherry and an orange slice.

VARIATIONS

■ Variations involve adding different regional flavors, such as the Tropical Sunrise (made with pineapple juice) or the Mango Sunrise (made with mango juice). You can always play around by adding different flavors until you find something you like.

■ The Tequila Sunrise is perhaps even more popular than the Vodka Sunrise and can be made (predictably) by substituting tequila in place of vodka (see page 216).

■ For a Virgin Sunrise, see page 217.

PEAR PRESSURE

We use the word "vanilla" as a code word for bland, but that isn't quite right. It's a more subtle flavor than, say, chocolate, but that's part of what makes it great. It's definitely what makes vanilla vodka great, and one of the reasons vanilla vodka and pear go together so well. Subtlety of flavor is what separates the pear from other fruits, and pairing it with vanilla makes for an understated drink you're sure to love.

BASIC INGREDIENTS

 1 part vanilla vodka

 1 part pear juice

 1 splash lime juice

 Sugar (for rimming)

 1 pear slice, thinly cut (garnish)

 GLASSWARE:
Old Fashioned glass.

1. Add the liquid ingredients to a cocktail shaker filled with ice and shake well.

2. Rim an Old Fashioned glass with sugar and strain the contents of the cocktail shaker into it.

3. Garnish with a thin slice of pear.

NEVER USED SUGAR OR SALT TO RIM THE EDGE OF A GLASS BEFORE?

It's easy. Although water will work just fine to make the sugar stick, you can add a little extra flavor by rubbing the edge of a lemon or lime along the rim of your glass instead. Then simply turn the glass over and press the rim into a bowl of sugar, salt, or whatever else you might be rimming the glass with. Presto! Added flavor, and beautiful presentation.

DRINK THE C

C is for Cointreau, that's good enough for me. But it helps to have a few more flavors in there, like cherry vodka, coconut rum, and cola, to round out the flavor profile of this C-heavy concoction. Is it a bit contrived for the sake of its name? Maybe. But it's also a delicious combination of flavors with a simple cola base, making this a simple, straightforward, and tasty cocktail fit for any occasion.

BASIC INGREDIENTS

I part cherry vodka

2 parts cola

I splash coconut rum

I splash Cointreau

 I maraschino cherry (garnish)

 GLASSWARE:
Old Fashioned glass.

1. Add ice, cherry vodka, and cola to your glass and stir together.

2. Top with a splash of coconut rum and Cointreau and stir again.

3. Garnish with a maraschino cherry.

MOCHA MOCHA MOCHA

Beware: This is a drink as dangerous as any out there. It is a mixture of sweet flavors so delicious that you're likely to forget that you're drinking something extremely strong. With three out of four ingredients containing alcohol, it's the sort of drink that might put you on the floor before you realize what's happened. Still, if flavor is what's most important (and I maintain that it is!), you won't do much better than this fantastic concoction.

BASIC INGREDIENTS

I part vodka

I part chocolate liqueur

I part coffee liqueur

2 parts milk

GLASSWARE:
Old Fashioned glass.

1. Add the vodka, liqueurs, and milk to a cocktail shaker filled with ice and shake vigorously.

2. Strain the resulting mixture into an Old Fashioned glass filled with ice.

GINGER BINGER

1 part vodka

1 splash triple sec

1 part grapefruit juice

2 parts ginger ale

1 lime wheel (garnish)

1 sprig mint (garnish)

Turn the page for the recipe!

→

GINGER BINGER

Ginger goes well with vodka, and while ginger beer is always a popular cocktail ingredient, ginger ale has none of the harsh bite that ginger beer all too often imparts to cocktails. Ginger ale, a subtle background upon which to build, allows other flavors to come forward and contribute to the cocktail's flavor profile, as the orange and grapefruit do here.

BASIC INGREDIENTS

I part vodka

I splash triple sec

I part grapefruit juice

2 parts ginger ale

I lime wheel (garnish)

I sprig mint (garnish)

GLASSWARE:
Highball glass.

1. Fill a highball glass with ice and add the vodka, triple sec, and grapefruit juice. Stir together.

2. Top with ginger ale and stir again. Garnish with a lime wheel and maybe even a sprig of mint.

VODKA NEGRONI

True, the Negroni is typically made with gin (find the classic Negroni recipe on page 162), but if all you've got is vodka, you can adapt it fairly easily. You can add a splash of crème de menthe to replace the notes of juniper provided by the gin and give the drink a little minty freshness. Just don't add too much, or it'll overwhelm the flavor of the drink. But all in all, this is a clever little spin on a classic cocktail.

BASIC INGREDIENTS:

I part vodka

I part Campari

I part sweet vermouth

I splash crème de menthe

I orange slice (garnish)

GLASSWARE:
Old Fashioned glass.

1. Fill a glass with ice and add the vodka, Campari, and sweet vermouth. Stir until thoroughly mixed.

2. Strain the resulting mixture into an Old Fashioned glass filled with ice.

3. Top with a splash of crème de menthe and garnish with an orange slice.

SAGE ADVICE

Kombucha is having a moment. For those who aren't familiar with this bubbly fermented tea, it is extremely versatile, coming in a wide range of forms and flavors. Many of these flavors go extremely well with alcohol—strawberry/sage in particular. If you can find this particular flavor of kombucha, give this delicious beverage a try. You'll find that the tartness of the kombucha plays nicely against the orange vodka, while sweet, smooth grenadine mellows everything out.

BASIC INGREDIENTS:

 I part orange vodka

 I part strawberry/sage Kombucha

 I part strawberry seltzer

 I splash grenadine

 I handful of sliced strawberries (garnish)

 GLASSWARE:
Highball glass.

1. Add the vodka, kombucha, and seltzer to a highball glass filled with ice.

2. Stir thoroughly.

3. Top with grenadine and sliced strawberries.

QUICKSLIDE

The Mudslide is a popular cocktail, but it's a little bit complicated. The Quickslide distills this classic drink down into a simple, easy-to-make cocktail that imparts the same great flavors you've come to expect from its more involved cousin. The Quickslide is perfect for large batches, whether you're serving guests at a backyard BBQ or just looking to cool down on the beach.

BASIC INGREDIENTS:

 I part vodka

 I part coffee liqueur

I part cream liqueur

Ice (as desired)

 I dusting cocoa powder (garnish)

GLASSWARE:
Cocktail glass.

1. Add the vodka, liqueurs, and ice to a blender. If you are using 1 oz. of each ingredient, 1 cup of ice will suffice. Note: Using more ice will create a thicker cocktail, and less ice will create a lighter cocktail.

2. Blend to desired consistency.

3. Pour the resulting mixture into a cocktail glass.

4. Garnish with a dusting of cocoa powder.

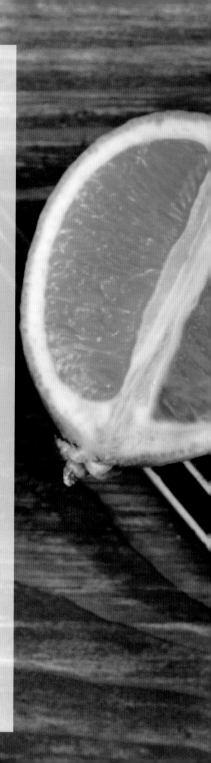

RUM

A more assertive flavor than vodka, rum tends to spring to the forefront of any drink it finds itself in. This is not a bad thing—the distinctive flavor of rum is something to build around rather than cover up. Some of the most famous rum cocktails are simply too complex to be included in a book of simple recipes. But maybe this is a blessing in disguise, forcing even the most seasoned rum drinker to step outside their comfort zone.

The Home Bartender, Second Edition is about making things easy on all of us. Why go to the store to gather the ingredients for something insanely complex when you can make a dozen simple cocktails with ingredients you probably already have? Whether it's the simple splash of grenadine in the Roses for Alex cocktail or the slightly more refined palate of the Daiquiri Twist, even the simplest rum drinks can offer a depth of flavor that other cocktails just can't match. Bust out the lime juice, check the pantry for sugar, and get ready for simple flavors everyone will love.

DAIQUIRI TWIST

This take on the classic daiquiri recipe substitutes a bit of triple sec for some of the white rum, taking down the intensity of the alcohol in favor of a more flavorful, drinkable cocktail. The Daiquiri Twist really lets the flavor of the rum shine without overwhelming your tongue with the taste of booze.

BASIC INGREDIENTS

 2 parts white rum

 1 part lime juice

 1 part triple sec

 1 splash simple syrup

 1 lime wheel (garnish)

 Sugar (for rimming)

GLASSWARE:
Cocktail glass.

1. Fill a cocktail shaker with ice and add the liquid ingredients. Shake well.

2. Rim a cocktail glass with sugar and strain the contents of the cocktail shaker into it.

3. Garnish with a lime wheel.

VARIATION

Everyone on earth has heard of the **strawberry daiquiri**, and you can make one by just adding a bit of strawberry schnapps in place of the triple sec. If you want the frozen version of the drink, add about half a cup of ice and blend it all together.

DON'T HAVE SIMPLE SYRUP? It's surprisingly easy to make. Simply add sugar and water to a pot in a 1:1 ratio, then bring it to a boil. When the cloudy mixture becomes completely clear, it's ready!

CUBA LIBRE

Another classic rum cocktail, the Cuba Libre is really little more than a standard rum and cola with a twist of lime and mint. That's not a negative—many of the best cocktails are the ones with simplest flavors. Why spend any more time than you have to mixing a drink, and why pretend that you need complex flavors for a beverage to be tasty? The Cuba Libre is the perfect answer to the complicated drinks favored by so many mixologists. No need to show off here. Flavor is all you need.

BASIC INGREDIENTS

 6 mint leaves

 1/2 lime (juiced)

 1 part white rum

 2 parts cola

 1 lime wedge (garnish)

GLASSWARE:
 Highball glass.

1. Tear the mint leaves in half and add them to the bottom of the highball glass. Add the lime juice and muddle together.

2. Add ice to the glass and pour in the rum and cola. Stir until thoroughly mixed.

3. Garnish with a lime wedge.

TROPICAL STORM

The Tropical Storm scales back the ever-popular Hurricane recipe into something a little more manageable for everyday consumption. After all, who keeps three types of rum on hand? The Tropical Storm maintains the flavors that make the Hurricane so beloved while decreasing its complexity, creating a cocktail you can easily make at home.

BASIC INGREDIENTS

 I part white rum

 I part dark rum

 I part passion fruit syrup

 1/2 lemon (juiced)

 I maraschino cherry (garnish)

GLASSWARE:
Hurricane glass.

1. Add the liquid ingredients to a cocktail shaker filled with ice and shake vigorously.

2. Strain the resulting mixture into a Hurricane glass.

3. Garnish with a maraschino cherry.

VARIATION

Part of what makes the **Hurricane** so popular is the inclusion of high-proof rum, which has been dropped in the slightly weaker Tropical Storm (get it?). If you really want that extra bit of boozy goodness in the drink, sub in some high-proof rum for the white rum.

SUNBURST

One of the great things about coconut rum is that its understated flavor doesn't force itself into the forefront quite as much as regular rum, allowing you to play off its subtler flavor a bit. It's also quite tasty in its own right. The Sunburst takes full advantage of this, mixing it with a few other tropical flavors to create a delicious burst of citrus with every sip.

BASIC INGREDIENTS

I part coconut rum

I part pineapple juice

I lemon wedge (juiced)

2 parts grapefruit juice

I grapefruit twist (garnish)

GLASSWARE:
Highball glass.

1. Add ice to your glass and add in the coconut rum, pineapple juice, and lemon juice.

2. Top with grapefruit juice and garnish with a grapefruit twist.

If you find yourself unable to make a perfect citrus twist, you can always just use a simple strip of zest. If you're intent on getting proper twists, though, there are tools you can purchase to make it easier.

YOUR TAI

A scaled-back version of the Mai Tai, Your Tai keeps most of the flavors that make the Mai Tai great while making it a little easier to mix at home. Eschewing the usual orgeat syrup, the drink still combines different rum flavors with Curaçao and lime juice to make a cocktail that is startlingly strong considering how easy it is to drink.

BASIC INGREDIENTS

 2 parts white rum

 1 part dark rum

 1 part Curaçao

 1/2 lime (juiced)

 1 orange slice (garnish)

 GLASSWARE:
Highball glass.

1. Add the rums, Curaçao, and lime juice to a cocktail shaker filled with ice and shake well.

2. Strain the resulting mixture into a highball glass filled with ice.

3. Garnish with an orange slice.

PIÑA COLADA

1 part white rum

1 part coconut milk

1 part triple sec

2 parts pineapple juice

Crushed ice (for blending)

1 pineapple wedge (garnish)

Turn the page for the recipe!

→

PIÑA COLADA

The Piña Colada is one of the most distinctively flavored cocktails. The coconut and pineapple combination might seem like an obvious one, but nobody has been able to outdo the tropical delight that is the Piña Colada. It's a fresh, creamy cocktail that's actually deceptively simple. For the speedy mixologist, we've added one ingredient—triple sec—to add an extra pop of freshness and keep the drink light.

BASIC INGREDIENTS

 I part white rum

 I part coconut milk

 I part triple sec

 2 parts pineapple juice

 Crushed ice (for blending)

 I pineapple wedge (garnish)

GLASSWARE:
Hurricane glass.

1. Add the white rum, coconut milk, triple sec, and pineapple juice to a blender with about ½ cup of ice. Blend until smooth.

2. Pour the resulting mixture into your glass and garnish with a pineapple wedge.

VIRGIN PIÑA COLADA

Piña Coladas are great, but too many of them can put you on the ground. Why not opt for the non-alcoholic option, containing the same great coconut and pineapple taste with none of the head-ringing aftereffects? The Virgin Piña Colada is a delicious, slushy drink guaranteed to leave you wanting more. Makes 4 servings.

BASIC INGREDIENTS

 1 part coconut cream

 3 parts pineapple juice

 2 to 4 cups crushed ice

 4 pineapple wedges (garnish)

 4 maraschino cherries (garnish)

GLASSWARE:
Hurricane glass.

1. Add coconut cream, pineapple juice, and ice to the blender and blend until smooth. Add as much ice as you want until you reach your desired consistency. It doesn't need to be too thick; when the ice melts, you don't want to leave yourself with a watered-down drink.

2. Pour into individual Hurricane glasses and garnish with pineapple wedges and cherries.

BANANA CREAM PIE

Vodka might pair well with cream, but rum pairs well with tropical fruits like the coconut and banana. There's just something about the flavor of rum that screams "beach." So why not blend up some bananas and cream for a thick, refreshing, smoothie-like drink that packs a potent punch of alcohol? The Banana Cream Pie is a unique and unusual cocktail that you're sure to love.

BASIC INGREDIENTS

 1 banana

 1 part vanilla rum

 1 part banana rum

 1 part cream

 1 dusting nutmeg (garnish)

 1 banana slice (garnish)

GLASSWARE:
Highball glass.

1. Cut one slice off the banana and reserve for a garnish.

2. Put the rest of the banana, vanilla rum, banana rum, and cream in a blender and blend until smooth.

3. Pour the resulting mixture into a highball glass and dust with a bit of nutmeg. Garnish with the banana circle.

CARIBBEAN
CRANBERRY TWIST

While rum is certainly tropical enough on its own, coconut rum can push any cocktail to the next level when it comes to Caribbean flavors. Enter the Caribbean Cranberry Twist, which accents the boozy goodness of coconut rum and triple sec with orange juice and cranberry juice. These light, fresh flavors will transport you straight to the beach no matter where you might be.

BASIC INGREDIENTS

1 part coconut rum

1 part orange juice

1 part cranberry juice

1 splash triple sec

1 orange slice (garnish)

GLASSWARE:
Highball glass.

1. Fill a highball glass with ice and add the rum, orange juice, and cranberry juice. Stir until thoroughly mixed.

2. Finish with a splash of triple sec and garnish with an orange slice.

RED RUM FIZZ

All of these rum drinks made with fruit juices and liqueurs are tasty, but they can get a little heavy after a while. Break it up by adding a little fizz to your life with the Red Rum Fizz. Heavy on the orange flavor, with a velvety red color thanks to the grenadine, the Red Rum Fizz is as beautiful as it is airy and delicious.

BASIC INGREDIENTS

 I part rum

 I part orange juice

 I part club soda

 I splash grenadine

 I maraschino cherry (garnish)

 I orange slice (garnish)

GLASSWARE:
Highball glass.

1. Mix the rum and orange juice together in a highball glass filled with ice.

2. Add club soda to fill.

3. Finish with a splash of grenadine and garnish with a maraschino cherry and an orange slice.

ONE DARK NIGHT

Ginger beer is a great ingredient to use in a huge number of cocktails, but tempering that harsh bite can be a bit of a challenge. Enter orgeat syrup, a delightfully almondy ingredient that adds a bit of nutty creaminess to any drink. With a bit of lime juice to elevate the drink, One Dark Night is perfect for any night.

 BASIC INGREDIENTS

I part dark rum

 2 parts ginger beer

 1/2 lime (juiced)

 I splash orgeat syrup

 I lime wedge (garnish)

 GLASSWARE:
Highball glass.

1. Add ice to a highball glass and pour in the rum, ginger beer, and lime juice. Stir until thoroughly mixed.

2. Finish with a splash of orgeat syrup. Do not stir.

3. Garnish with a wedge of lime.

CIDERMEISTER

More coconut rum? Naturally! Jägermeister may have a reputation for being the chosen drink of college students everywhere, but anyone can enjoy this unique spiced liquor. When paired with something a bit more subtle, like coconut rum, it can actually add quite a bit of flavor to any drink. Apple cider is best when spiced anyway, making Jägermeister the perfect mixing agent for the delicious and unique Cidermeister drink.

BASIC INGREDIENTS

 I part coconut rum

 I part Jägermeister

 4 parts fresh apple cider

 I dusting cinnamon

 I cinnamon stick (garnish)

 GLASSWARE:
Highball glass.

1. Add ice to a highball glass and pour in the coconut rum, Jägermeister, and apple cider. Stir until thoroughly mixed.

2. Finish with a dusting of cinnamon. Add a cinnamon stick for garnish.

VANILLA FLOAT

Have you ever noticed that when you add spiced rum to cola, the result tastes a little bit like vanilla? Well, there is no reason not to take full advantage of that and add a scoop of ice cream to boot. It's so simple you'll be kicking yourself for not thinking of it before!

BASIC INGREDIENTS

 I part spiced rum

 2 parts cola

 I scoop vanilla ice cream

 GLASSWARE:
Pint glass.

1. Pour the spiced rum and cola into a pint glass.

2. Add a scoop of vanilla ice cream, and serve with a long spoon.

VARIATIONS

Ice cream floats can be made in many different ways, so feel free to choose any flavor combination you like. If you'd rather make it with root beer and coconut ice cream, go for it! You might even sub in orange soda if you're feeling particularly adventurous. For an added bit of sweetness, rim the glass with sugar so you'll have something extra to enjoy when you slurp down what's left.

SPICED TEA

What could be better than a glass of iced tea on a hot summer day? How about Spiced Tea? Spiking your iced tea with a splash of spiced rum and adding a bit of lemon and mint can go a long way toward developing the complex-but-simple flavors you deserve. Why settle for less when having more is so easy?

BASIC INGREDIENTS

 6 mint leaves

 1/2 lemon (juiced)

 1 part spiced rum

 2 parts iced tea

 1 lemon wheel (garnish)

 GLASSWARE:
Highball glass.

1. Tear the mint leaves in half and add them to the bottom of your glass. Add the lemon juice and muddle them together.

2. Add ice, then add the spiced rum and iced tea. Stir until thoroughly mixed.

3. Garnish with a lemon wheel.

COOL SUMMER

20 mint leaves

4 lime wedges (juiced)

1 part white rum

2 parts lemonade

4 lemon wheels (garnish)

Turn the page for the recipe!
⟶

COOL SUMMER

The great thing about lemonade is how easy it is to mix with just about any liquor. Vodka, gin, rum... even whiskey mixes just fine with that greatest of all summer drinks. So add a little rum to your lemonade, add in a little extra citrus, and cool down with a refreshing Cool Summer cocktail. Make it by the pitcher and share with your friends! Makes 4 servings.

BASIC INGREDIENTS

 20 mint leaves

 4 lime wedges (juiced)

 1 part white rum

 2 parts lemonade

 4 lemon wheels (garnish)

GLASSWARE:
Highball glass.

1. Tear the mint leaves in half and add them to a pitcher. Juice the lime wedges into the pitcher and muddle the ingredients together as best you can.

2. Add ice, rum, and lemonade. Stir until thoroughly mixed.

3. Pour into individual glasses and garnish with lemon wheels.

AFTER DARK

The After Dark is essentially a pomegranate Italian soda with a dash of bitters and a healthy dose of rum, and doesn't that just sound fantastic? It's sweet and light, but also dark and bitter. It offers a medley of different flavors that dance across your tongue.

BASIC INGREDIENTS

 I part dark rum

 2 parts club soda

 I splash pomegranate syrup

 2 drops bitters

 I maraschino cherry (garnish)

 I orange wedge (garnish)

 GLASSWARE:
Old Fashioned glass.

1. Add ice to an Old Fashioned glass. Pour in the dark rum and top with club soda.

2. Add a splash of pomegranate syrup and let it settle into the club soda. Finish with two drops of bitters.

3. Garnish with a maraschino cherry and an orange wedge.

ROSES FOR ALEX

Another drink on the lighter side of things, Roses for Alex plays the nice orange flavor of triple sec off a bit of white rum. The bright red color added by the grenadine will shine through, making you think of a dozen roses for someone you love.

BASIC INGREDIENTS

 I part white rum

 I part triple sec

 2 parts club soda

 I splash grenadine

 I maraschino cherry (garnish)

 GLASSWARE:
Old Fashioned glass.

1. Fill an Old Fashioned glass with ice, then add the white rum and triple sec. Top with club soda.

2. Finish with a splash of grenadine. Garnish with a maraschino cherry.

FOUR FELLOWS

There are so many different kinds of rum, and some of them go quite well together. Many drinks make use of both white and dark rum, but how about the four most popular kinds of rum all together in one delicious shot? Whether shots are your thing or not, sometimes it's nice to combine a bunch of competing flavors together and just see what happens. The Four Fellows shot gives you this opportunity, and you might be surprised at just how easily it goes down.

BASIC INGREDIENTS

 I part white rum

 I part dark rum

 I part spiced rum

 I part coconut rum

 GLASSWARE:
Shot glass.

1. Pour the four rums into a shot glass in roughly equal proportions. You can try to layer them if you like, but it will be a challenge.

VARIATION

If you want something a little stronger (you're a braver person than I), omit the coconut rum in favor of a high-proof rum such as Bacardi 151. You'll lose some flavor, but it will definitely add a good deal of kick to an already strong drink.

CUBAN REDHEAD

1 part white rum

1 part coffee liqueur

1 part Irish cream

1 dash crème de menthe

1 mint sprig (garnish)

Turn the page for the recipe!

→

CUBAN REDHEAD

Rum and Irish cream aren't exactly a common mixture, but you might be surprised at how well they go together, especially with a bit of coffee liqueur to offset them. The addition of a dash of crème de menthe elevates this Irish-Cuban hybrid into something truly remarkable. Just watch your intake—this is a strong one.

BASIC INGREDIENTS

 I part white rum

 I part coffee liqueur

 I part Irish cream

 I dash crème de menthe

 I mint sprig (garnish)

GLASSWARE:
 Old Fashioned glass.

1. Add the rum, coffee liqueur, and Irish cream to a cocktail shaker filled with ice. Shake vigorously.

2. Strain the resulting mixture into an Old Fashioned glass over ice. Top with a dash of crème de menthe.

3. Garnish with a mint sprig.

CUBAN COFFEE

Irish Coffee is the famous mixture of Irish whiskey, coffee, and Irish cream, so it only makes sense that Cuban Coffee would feature Cuban rum. Cuban Coffee is a great cocktail for when you want to whisk away a hangover from the night before. With caffeine to keep you awake and a splash of booze to give you a buzz, it's hard to go wrong with this delicious cocktail.

BASIC INGREDIENTS

 I part dark Cuban rum

 3 parts coffee

 I spoonful sugar

 I splash cream liqueur

 **GLASSWARE:**
Irish Coffee glass.

1. Pour the rum and coffee into an Irish Coffee glass and stir together.

2. Add a spoonful of sugar and a dash of cream liqueur. Stir again until thoroughly mixed.

PRIVATEER

1/2 lime (juiced)

1 part coconut rum

3 parts cola

1 lime wedge (garnish)

Turn the page for the recipe!

PRIVATEER

You don't need to do anything too fancy to maximize the deliciousness of coconut rum, and the Privateer proves it. With just a little coconut rum and lime, regular old cola becomes a culinary delight, dancing across your taste buds with a bubbly, fizzy airiness that packs a flavorful punch.

BASIC INGREDIENTS

 1/2 lime (juiced)

 I part coconut rum

 3 parts cola

 I lime wedge (garnish)

GLASSWARE:
Highball glass.

1. Squeeze the lime juice into your glass.

2. Add ice as desired, then add the rum and cola. Stir until mixed.

3. Garnish with a lime wedge.

VIRGIN PRIVATEER

Lime and cola are good, but adding a little bit of coconut flavor is better. You've probably had coconut coffee or maybe even a coconut Italian soda, but the Virgin Privateer takes that great coconut flavor and uses it to accent lime and cola. The drink has a surprisingly complex flavor profile for something so easy to make, and you're sure to love it!

BASIC INGREDIENTS

 1/2 lime (juiced)

 1 oz. coconut syrup

 8 oz. cola

 1 lemon wheel (garnish)

 GLASSWARE:
Highball glass.

1. Squeeze the lime juice into your glass.

2. Add ice, then add the coconut syrup and cola. Stir until mixed.

3. Garnish with a lemon wheel.

ISLAND PUNCH

Here's a tasty drink that absolutely anyone can enjoy. A little Island Punch takes the distinct flavor of dark rum and pits it against sweet, tangy pineapple and orange juices. The drops of bitters add a little bit of depth to this cocktail.

BASIC INGREDIENTS

 I part dark rum

 I part pineapple juice

 I part orange juice

 2 drops bitters

 I pineapple slice (garnish)

GLASSWARE:
Pint glass.

1. Add the rum, juices, and bitters to a cocktail shaker filled with ice. Shake well.

2. Strain the resulting mixture into a pint glass filled with ice.

3. Garnish with a slice of pineapple.

RUMMAGE SALE

No doubt many of you will be familiar with the idea of a rummage sale. A little of this, a little of that — the junk you've accumulated over the years, tossed into the yard for someone else to buy. This cocktail captures the spirit of the rummage sale: whatever you've got in your cabinets, toss it in! Rum? Great! Mint? Awesome! Lemon juice? Squeeze it in! The Rummage Sale cocktail embraces the spirit of ingenuity...and the beauty of improvisation. It works with just about any flavor, and the result will be something to be proud of.

BASIC INGREDIENTS:

 I part rum

 2 parts seltzer (any flavor)

 I squeeze lemon juice

 or 3 mint leaves (or I dash crème de menthe)

GLASSWARE:
Highball glass.

1. Muddle the mint and lemon juice in the bottom of a highball glass.

2. Add the rum and seltzer.

3. Fill glass with ice and stir thoroughly. Garnish with mint leaves.

ROYAL RUM-BOWL

Let's get ready for a rum bowl! This is a way-too-boozy concoction featuring three different types of booze offset by not much more than a bit of grenadine. Sometimes you want to taste the booze you're drinking, and this is one of those times. The rum, whiskey, and brandy mix well, each bringing a different element to the glass. The muted flavor of the grenadine brings them all together, its fruity flavor complemented by the maraschino cherry garnish. Feel free to splash in a little of the maraschino cherry juice, too.

BASIC INGREDIENTS:

 I part rum

 I part Crown Royal whiskey

 I part brandy

 I splash grenadine

 I maraschino cherry (garnish)

 GLASSWARE:
Old Fashioned glass.

1. Add the rum, whiskey, brandy, and grenadine to a cocktail shaker filled with ice.

2. Shake well.

3. Strain the resulting mixture into an Old Fashioned glass filled with ice.

4. Garnish with a maraschino cherry.

MOJITO EXPRESS

A traditional mojito is a fairly complicated cocktail, but for the purposes of this book we've distilled it down to four core ingredients: rum, seltzer, simple syrup, and mint. After all, why go all out with all kinds of different ingredients when you can make a perfectly tasty substitute with just four? Mojito purists may turn their noses up at the idea, but most people will find this drink to be a tasty alternative.

BASIC INGREDIENTS:

 1 part white rum

 2 parts lime seltzer

 1 splash simple syrup

 6 mint leaves

 1 lime wheel (garnish)

GLASSWARE:
Highball glass.

1. Muddle the mint leaves and simple syrup in the bottom of a highball glass, then add ice.

2. Add the rum and seltzer.

3. Stir until thoroughly mixed.

4. Garnish with a lime wheel.

MAPLE CREAMER

Breakfast: the most important meal of the day. Who doesn't love waffles and syrup, with a nice cold glass of milk on the side? The Maple Creamer evokes all the flavors of this classic breakfast, combining maple syrup with a little rum and cream to create a beverage that goes down nice and smooth.

BASIC INGREDIENTS:

 I part maple syrup

 2 parts Irish cream

 I part rum

 I part milk or cream

GLASSWARE:
Cocktail glass.

1. Add maple syrup, Irish cream, rum, and milk or cream to a cocktail shaker filled with ice.

2. Shake vigorously.

3. Strain the resulting mixture into a cocktail glass.

ALMOND RUM SPLASH

Orgeat syrup is a delicious and underused ingredient. It has a smooth, rich, almond flavor that most people recognize from the Mai Tai cocktail. But this syrup actually has a variety of uses, and pairs well with rum in almost any instance. The Almond Rum Splash is something of a cross between a Mai Tai and a Mojito, featuring the best qualities of each.

BASIC INGREDIENTS:

 2 parts rum

 2 parts club soda

 1 part orgeat syrup

 3 mint leaves

 1 lemon wheel (garnish)

GLASSWARE:
Highball glass.

1. Fill a pint glass with ice and add the rum and club soda. Stir thoroughly.

2. In a highball glass, muddle the orgeat syrup and the mint leaves.

3. Add ice to the highball glass and strain in the rum-and-club soda mixture. Stir together.

4. Garnish with a lemon wheel.

SPICE CAKE

Spice cakes are great in the fall—especially when they have a little apple filling. The Spice Cake cocktail takes that great apple taste and combines it with spiced rum to build layers of flavor that recall a crisp fall day. A little cinnamon and simple syrup give the drink a sweet and aromatic finish.

BASIC INGREDIENTS:

 I part spiced rum

 2 parts apple juice

 I dash simple syrup

 I dusting cinnamon

 I cinnamon stick (garnish)

GLASSWARE:
Cocktail glass.

1. Combine the rum, apple juice, simple syrup, and cinnamon in a cocktail shaker filled with ice.

2. Shake vigorously.

3. Strain the resulting mixture into a cocktail glass.

4. Garnish with a cinnamon stick.

LOGAN'S RUM

This is a beautiful, ruby red cocktail that smuggles two different types of rum beneath a cozy blanket of cranberry. White rum and coconut rum work well together, and the tropical coconut flavor balances the tartness of the cranberry. The citrusy punch of the lime ties everything together.

BASIC INGREDIENTS:

 I part white rum

 I part coconut rum

 3 parts cranberry juice

 I dash lime juice

 I lime wedge (garnish)

GLASSWARE:
Cocktail glass.

1. Add the white rum, coconut rum, lime juice, and cranberry juice to a cocktail shaker filled with ice.

2. Shake vigorously.

3. Strain the resulting mixture into a cocktail glass.

4. Garnish with a lime wedge.

GIN

Ah, gin. The bite of alcohol combined with the freshness of juniper tastes like Christmas to me. Those who love gin tend to love the scent of pine, the clear crispness of the liquid, and how well it pairs with simple ingredients like club soda and lime. Gin is a great addition to a great many cocktails, but what makes it great is how well it can stand on its own. The gin martini is one of the most famous gin drinks around, and most versions contain no more than two or three ingredients. After all, why muddle the taste of gin when it's already so delicious? And let's not forget the Gin and Tonic (or its buffed up cousin, the 1505 G&T)—a drink so delicious that it needs naught but a hint of fizz and a bit of lime to push it over the top.

Whereas harsher liquors like vodka tend to need extra ingredients to prop them up, gin cocktails are remarkable in how well they complement the existing flavor of the gin. You should never feel the need to drown the flavor of gin, and this basic rule allows the principle behind *The Home Bartender, Second Edition* to shine. Nothing complex. Nothing over-the-top. Nothing that muddles a dozen different flavors until you can barely remember which liquor you started with. No, gin is a liquor that deserves respect, and keeping your ingredients list short is the best way to show it.

CLASSIC MARTINI

Ah, the martini. A classic beverage, celebrated through the ages by cocktail aficionados, famous writers, and, of course, that most famous of fictional British spies. The Classic Martini is simple, straightforward, and delicious, with nary a wasted ingredient. If you've never made yourself a martini, now is the time.

BASIC INGREDIENTS:

4 parts Tanqueray gin

1 part dry vermouth

1 lemon twist (garnish)

GLASSWARE:
Cocktail glass.

1. Add the gin and vermouth to a cocktail shaker filled with ice.

2. Shake vigorously.

3. Strain the resulting mixture into a cocktail glass.

4. Garnish with a twist of lemon.

DIRTY MARTINI

The standard martini is great, but the Dirty Martini adds a little extra brine that really brings out the flavor of the dry vermouth. Many have asked what business olives have being such an integral part of a popular cocktail. The truth is, no one knows who first thought to add olives to a martini, but they were undeniably on to something.

BASIC INGREDIENTS:

 4 parts gin

 1 part dry vermouth

 1 splash olive brine

 3 pimento-stuffed olives (garnish)

 GLASSWARE:
Cocktail glass.

1. Add the gin, vermouth, and olive brine to a cocktail shaker filled with ice. Shake vigorously.

2. Strain the resulting mixture into a cocktail glass.

3. Garnish with three olives on a toothpick.

BUDGET MARTINI

One of the great things about gin is that most people have a hard time differentiating between the flavor of expensive gin and the flavor of cheap gin. This might be bad for the gin industry, but for the shrewd customer it's actually a boon. You can make yourself a delicious Budget Martini without breaking the bank, and be confident that it will taste almost exactly as good as a top-shelf version.

BASIC INGREDIENTS:

 4 parts New Amsterdam gin

 1 part dry vermouth

 1 dash lemon juice

 GLASSWARE:
Cocktail glass.

1. Add the gin and vermouth to a cocktail shaker filled with ice. Shake vigorously.

2. Strain the resulting mixture into a cocktail glass.

3. Add a tiny squeeze of lemon juice.

Don't have a cocktail glass? No worries! The martini is a versatile cocktail, and you might find you enjoy it even more on the rocks in an Old Fashioned glass. The choice is yours!

THE FILTHY ASSISTANT

You've heard of a Dirty Martini? The Filthy Assistant puts a spin on the idea, swapping salty and briny for fresh and herbal, a switch that breathes new life into the recipe and gives gin lovers something new to reach for.

BASIC INGREDIENTS:

 4 parts gin

 1 part dry vermouth

 6 mint leaves

 1-3 cocktail onions (garnish)

GLASSWARE:
Cocktail glass.

1. Add gin, vermouth, and 3 mint leaves to a cocktail shaker filled with ice.

2. Shake vigorously.

3. Strain the resulting mixture into a cocktail glass.

4. Garnish with the remaining 3 mint leaves and a few cocktail onions on a toothpick.

WAKEUP MARTINI

When you wake up in the morning, your first thought might not be of booze. But on a lazy Saturday morning, why shouldn't it be? The Wakeup Martini is the perfect breakfast cocktail, separating itself from traditional morning drinks like the Bloody Mary or Irish Coffee by adding breakfast flavors like maple and orange.

BASIC INGREDIENTS

 2 parts gin

 1 part triple sec

 1 splash lemon juice

 1 splash maple syrup

 1 lemon twist (garnish)

GLASSWARE:
Cocktail glass.

1. Pour the liquid ingredients into a cocktail shaker with ice and shake well to completely integrate the maple syrup.

2. Strain the resulting mixture into a cocktail glass. Garnish with a lemon twist.

ORANGE MARTINI

Martinis are delicious, but maybe a bit too simple? Add a bit of extra flavor with the Orange Martini, a delicious mixture of the standard martini flavor and citrus's bite. A little bit of blood orange liqueur goes a long way here, both in terms of imparting flavor and adding brightness to a typically colorless cocktail.

BASIC INGREDIENTS

 3 parts gin

 I part dry vermouth

 I part blood orange liqueur

 I dash orange bitters

 I orange twist (garnish)

 GLASSWARE:
Cocktail glass.

1. Add the gin, vermouth, liqueur, and bitters to a mixing glass filled with ice and stir until thoroughly mixed.

2. Strain the resulting mixture into a cocktail glass. Garnish with an orange twist.

VARIATION

Of course, you could make a similar cocktail with any flavor you prefer. Orange is one of the best because of the unique coloration of the blood orange liqueur, but you could concoct a similar drink using cherry liqueur, watermelon liqueur, or any other flavor you've taken a shine to.

MARTINI SHOOTER

This mini martini packs all of the drink's classic flavor into a single gulp. Is it classy? Is it not? In this case, the answer is probably in the eye of the beholder (or the drinker). Gin generally isn't the most popular liquor to shoot, but the Martini Shooter offers a delicious and, well, weirdly adorable way to develop a taste for it.

BASIC INGREDIENTS

 1 oz. gin

 1/4 oz. dry vermouth

 1 dash olive brine

 1 pimento-stuffed olive

 GLASSWARE:
Shot glass.

1. Mix the ingredients together in a shot glass. Add one pimento-stuffed green olive to the bottom of the glass.

2. Throw it back and don't forget to eat the olive—it's an essential part of the experience.

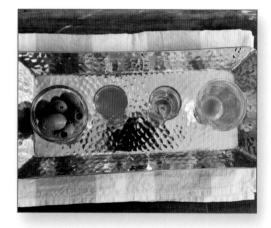

CLASSIC
GIN AND TONIC

1 part Tanqueray gin

1 part tonic water

1 splash lime juice

1 lime wedge (garnish)

Turn the page for the recipe!

→

CLASSIC GIN AND TONIC

Always start simple. The gin and tonic is a classic cocktail that you can order in any bar or make for yourself at home. "But," you're probably thinking, "isn't a gin and tonic just gin and tonic?" All right, you've got me there. But the best part about starting with such a simple cocktail is that it has the sort of nice, clean look that classes up any occasion.

 BASIC INGREDIENTS

 I part Tanqueray gin

 I part tonic water

 I splash lime juice

 I lime wedge (garnish)

GLASSWARE:
Old Fashioned glass.

1. Fill a glass with ice and pour in the gin and tonic water. Stir until thoroughly mixed.

2. Top with a splash of lime juice. Garnish with a lime wedge.

PERFECT GIN AND TONIC

Believe it or not, you actually can improve on the Classic Gin and Tonic. Start by using some top-shelf gin. This recipe calls for Bombay Sapphire, but you can certainly substitute a gin such as Hendrick's if it suits you better. Also, try to tease an extra bit of flavor out of the fresh ingredients by muddling the lime juice with some fresh lime in your glass. You won't be disappointed with the results.

BASIC INGREDIENTS

 I splash lime juice

 I lime wheel (muddled)

 I part Bombay Sapphire gin

 I part tonic water

 I lime wheel (garnish)

GLASSWARE:
Old Fashioned glass.

1. Muddle a lime wheel and fresh lime juice at the bottom of your glass. Add ice.

2. Pour in the gin and top with tonic water. Stir until thoroughly mixed.

3. Garnish with another lime wheel.

BUDGET GIN AND TONIC

There's nothing wrong with cheaper gins like Gordon's or Seagram's. In fact, lower-shelf gin tends to be better than the lower-shelf options for other liquors. So while you might balk at the Budget Gin and Tonic, there's really no reason to do so. It might be a bit harsher than the smooth, velvety taste achieved by more expensive gins, but it lacks none of the flavor.

BASIC INGREDIENTS

 I part Seagram's gin

 I part tonic water

 I splash lime juice

 I lime wedge (garnish)

 GLASSWARE:
Old Fashioned glass.

1. Fill a glass with ice and pour in the gin and tonic water. Stir until thoroughly mixed. Top with a splash of lime juice.

2. Garnish with a lime wedge.

1505 G&T

Maybe though, just maybe, what makes the gin and tonic special to you is the fact that it's just so drinkable. Maybe what makes the gin and tonic your go-to drink is the fact that you can make one as big as you want and sip on it for the next hour or two, confident that the first sip will be just as delicious as the last. Well then, the 1505 G&T is for you. Named for the address of its Connecticut waterfront birthplace, it'll keep a drink in your hand for the next hour or more, and it's the perfect way to start or end the night.

BASIC INGREDIENTS

2 parts Tanqueray gin

I part lime juice (fresh)

4 parts tonic water

GLASSWARE:
24 oz. tumbler.

1. Fill your tumbler about ¼ of the way with gin, then add ice.

2. Add the lime juice, then top off with tonic water.

3. Stir until thoroughly mixed.

NOT-QUITE COLLINS

One of the most popular (and tasty) gin drinks is the Tom Collins, but the typical amount of sugar makes it a little bit sweet for our taste. No matter—it's an easy drink to adapt in a variety of different ways! Dropping the usual dose of sugar leaves us with something that isn't quite a Tom Collins... but is just as tasty.

 BASIC INGREDIENTS

1 part gin

 1 tsp. sugar

1 splash lemon juice

2 parts club soda

1 orange slice (garnish)

1 maraschino cherry (garnish)

GLASSWARE:
Collins glass or Highball glass.

1. Add the gin, sugar, and lemon juice to a cocktail shaker filled with ice and shake until thoroughly mixed.

2. Strain the resulting mixture into a Collins or highball glass. Top with club soda.

3. Garnish with an orange slice and a maraschino cherry.

VARIATION

As there are Tom Collins recipes that use lemon or lime juice, feel free to use the one you prefer. Only have lime juice? No worries. The flavors are slightly different but equally tasty.

NEGRONI

Speaking of gorgeous drinks, you probably won't find a better looking cocktail than the Negroni. Sporting a deep red hue courtesy of the sweet vermouth and Campari it prominently features, the Negroni is a delicious, gin-based answer to the famous Manhattan whiskey cocktail. Want to put a little twist on this classic cocktail? Try finishing with a dash of bitters.

BASIC INGREDIENTS

 1 part gin

 1 part Campari

 1 part sweet vermouth

 1 dash bitters

 1 orange slice (garnish)

 GLASSWARE:
Old Fashioned glass.

1. Add the liquid ingredients to a glass filled with ice and stir until thoroughly mixed.

2. Strain the resulting mixture into an Old Fashioned glass over ice. Garnish with an orange slice.

GIN ROSE

Similar to the Roses for Alex, the Gin Rose is a brightly colored cocktail that attains a perfect level of airiness. With a slight orange twist against the boldness of the gin, the Gin Rose is a sweet little beverage with a gorgeous red color.

BASIC INGREDIENTS

 I part gin

 I part triple sec

 2 parts club soda

 I splash grenadine

 I maraschino cherry (garnish)

 GLASSWARE:
Old Fashioned glass.

1. Pour the gin and triple sec into an Old Fashioned glass filled with ice. Add club soda to fill and stir until thoroughly mixed.

2. Top with a splash of grenadine. Garnish with a maraschino cherry.

SALTY MUTT

Similar to the popular salty dog, the Salty Mutt adds another flavor to the equation by cutting the grapefruit juice with cranberry juice. There's sticking with what works and then there's branching out into a whole new set of flavors. The salty dog may be an old friend, but the Salty Mutt is a boozy companion you can count on.

BASIC INGREDIENTS

 Salt (for rimming)

 1 part gin

 1 part grapefruit juice

 1 part cranberry juice

 1 grapefruit wedge (garnish)

 GLASSWARE: Old Fashioned glass.

1. Rim the glass with salt.

2. Add the gin, grapefruit juice, and cranberry juice to a cocktail shaker filled with ice. Shake vigorously.

3. Strain the resulting mixture over ice into an Old Fashioned glass—or highball glass if you're extra thirsty.

4. Garnish with a grapefruit wedge.

SINGAPORE EXPRESS

The Singapore Sling is an astoundingly tasty cocktail, but man is it complicated. By toning down the complexity of the flavors just a little bit, you can still whip up a fantastic cocktail that captures the essence of the Singapore Sling and doesn't take all day. All you need is a handful of ingredients and a set of taste buds.

BASIC INGREDIENTS

 2 parts gin

 1 part cherry liqueur

 1 part triple sec

 3 parts pineapple juice

 1 maraschino cherry (garnish)

 1 orange slice (garnish)

GLASSWARE:
Hurricane glass.

1. Pour the gin, liqueur, triple sec, and pineapple juice into a cocktail shaker filled with ice and shake vigorously.

2. Strain the resulting mixture into a Hurricane glass filled with ice.

3. Garnish with a maraschino cherry and a slice of orange.

HINT OF MINT

This fizzy ginger ale-and-lemonade concoction is the perfect punch for any large gathering. Just fill a punch bowl with ice and let guests go to town on this refreshing alternative to boring old fruit punches. The addition of a few mint leaves will add a subtle hint of flavor that will make partygoers say "Mmm, what is that?" *Makes 4 servings.*

BASIC INGREDIENTS

 20 mint leaves

 1 part ginger ale

 2 parts lemonade

 1 part gin

 4 lemon wheels (garnish)

GLASSWARE:
 Highball or pint glasses.

1. Tear the mint leaves in half and add them to the bottom of a pitcher. Add ice.

2. Pour in the ginger ale, lemonade, and gin, and stir until mixed.

3. Serve in individual glasses and garnish with lemon wheels.

GIN AND JUICE

Sporting a trio of delicious fruit flavors along with the usual juniper of the gin, Gin and Juice is a delicious alternative to a simple gin and cranberry combination. The addition of triple sec and lime juice gives the drink something of a fruit salad feel, making this a delicious and fresh-tasting drink that is perfect for any time of year.

 BASIC INGREDIENTS

 1 part gin

 1 part cranberry juice

 1 splash triple sec

 1/2 lime (juiced)

 1 lime wheel (garnish)

GLASSWARE:
Old Fashioned glass.

1. Add the gin, cranberry juice, triple sec, and lime juice to a cocktail shaker filled with ice and shake vigorously.

2. Strain the resulting mixture into an Old Fashioned glass containing your desired amount of ice.

3. Garnish with a lime wheel.

CHERRY GIN SOUR

There are a lot of great sour cocktails out there, but few of them contain gin. This is a shame, because, while you might not think of juniper as the perfect taste to complement a sour cocktail, gin can rise to the challenge of any flavor you pit against it. The Cherry Gin Sour is an excellent proof of this concept, as the flavor of the gin perfectly accents the cherry and lemon.

BASIC INGREDIENTS

 1 part gin

 1 part cherry liqueur

 1 part lemon juice

 1 splash simple syrup

 1 maraschino cherry (garnish)

 1 orange slice (garnish)

 GLASSWARE:
Old Fashioned glass.

1. Add the gin, cherry liqueur, lemon juice, and simple syrup to a cocktail shaker filled with ice and shake well.

2. Strain the resulting mixture into an Old Fashioned glass filled with ice.

3. Garnish with a maraschino cherry and an orange slice.

CLASSIC GIMLET

4 oz. Tanqueray gin

1/2 lime (juiced)

1 lime wheel (garnish)

Turn the page for the recipe!

CLASSIC GIMLET

The gimlet is as classic as it gets. Featuring just two ingredients (gin and lime), the gimlet is gin's sour answer to the martini. Easy to make and even easier to drink, the Classic Gimlet balances half a lime's worth of juice against four ounces of gin. Garnished with a lime wheel, the Classic Gimlet features fresh flavors that will never go out of style.

BASIC INGREDIENTS

4 oz. Tanqueray gin

1/2 lime (juiced)

1 lime wheel (garnish)

GLASSWARE:
Cocktail glass.

1. Add the gin to a cocktail shaker filled with ice along with the lime juice. Shake until thoroughly mixed.

2. Strain the resulting mixture into a cocktail glass.

3. Garnish with a lime wheel.

TWISTED GIMLET

The traditional gimlet is a classic combination of flavors, but the Twisted Gimlet asks, "What if we could do better?" Whether the Twisted Gimlet surpasses its originator is up to you, but it certainly offers something different. The addition of orange bitters in particular differentiates it in a unique and delicious way.

BASIC INGREDIENTS

 2 parts gin

 1 part triple sec

 1 part lime juice

 2 drops orange bitters

 1 lime wheel (garnish)

 GLASSWARE:
Cocktail glass.

1. Add the liquid ingredients to a mixing glass filled with ice. Stir until thoroughly mixed.

2. Strain the resulting mixture into a cocktail glass.

3. Garnish with a lime wheel.

GIN WATERFALL

A little champagne and a little Sprite complement gin quite well, creating a party punch perfect for any get together. Of course, the best part of a punch is that you can control the strength—dial it back if you're concerned about your guests getting too drunk, or kick it up a notch if you're gearing up for a long night! *Makes 10 servings.*

BASIC INGREDIENTS

 1 part gin

 1 part champagne

 2 parts Sprite

 5 lemons (juiced)

 20 lemon wheels
(garnish, punch bowl)

 GLASSWARE:
Highball glasses.

1. Add all the liquid ingredients together in a large punch bowl.

2. Stir together until thoroughly mixed, then add several lemons' worth of lemon wheels as a garnish. Ladle into highball glasses filled with ice.

MAKING A LARGE-BATCH DRINK?

Fruit slices—especially fruit wheels—are a great way to add a little extra character to your presentation. Cut a few oranges, limes, lemons, or other fruits into rounds and add them to your pitcher or punch bowl for a look that's sure to impress.

GIN POM POM

6 mint leaves

1 part gin

1 part pomegranate juice

1 lime wedge (juiced)

1 lime wheel (garnish)

Turn the page for the recipe!

GIN
POM POM

Pomegranate is an extremely underrated cocktail ingredient. Come to think of it, pomegranate is an extremely underrated fruit (probably because the only thing harder than retrieving the edible part is winning a land war in Asia). So forget the fruit itself—focus on the juice and make yourself a delicious Gin Pom Pom. With a splash of lime juice and a hint of mint, this is a drink that truly elevates its components.

BASIC INGREDIENTS

6 mint leaves

1 part gin

1 part pomegranate juice

1 lime wedge (juiced)

1 lime wheel (garnish)

GLASSWARE:
Old Fashioned glass.

1. Tear the mint leaves in half and add them to a cocktail shaker filled with ice. Add the gin, pomegranate juice, and juice from a lime wedge and shake well.

2. Strain the resulting mixture into an Old Fashioned glass filled with ice.

3. Garnish with a lime wheel.

FRENCH 75

The French 75 isn't as prominent as it once was, but if you've had one, chances are it has made its way onto your list of favorite cocktails. Gin and champagne are such an elegant combination—the fizz of the champagne is a sweet and flavorful alternative to the club soda and tonic water that gin typically finds itself paired with. This is one drink where the garnish actually makes the drink; if you don't serve it with a lemon twist and a cherry balanced over the glass on a toothpick, you've done it wrong.

BASIC INGREDIENTS

 I sugar cube

 I lemon wedge (juiced)

 I part gin

 2 parts champagne

 I lemon twist (garnish)

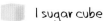 I skewered cherry (garnish)

 GLASSWARE:
Champagne flute.

1. Add a sugar cube to your champagne flute and squeeze in the juice from one lemon wedge.

2. Pour in the gin and top with champagne.

3. Garnish with a lemon twist. Skewer a cherry with a toothpick and place it over the top of the champagne flute.

VIRGIN 75

Just because it's your turn to be the designated driver doesn't mean that you shouldn't be able to take part in the festivities! The French 75 (page 185) is a classy cocktail, perfect for special occasions. The Virgin 75 captures its distinct look, right down to the color and the slowly dissolving sugar cube. Join your friends and sip away!

BASIC INGREDIENTS:

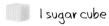 I sugar cube

 I part lemon juice

4 parts ginger ale

I lemon twist (garnish)

GLASSWARE:
Champagne flute.

1. Place a sugar cube at the bottom of a champagne flute.

2. Add the lemon juice, then the ginger ale.

3. Garnish with a twist of lemon.

BLUEBERRY SPARKLER

2 oz. gin

1 oz. blueberry simple syrup

1/2 lemon (juiced)

1 oz. club soda

1 lemon wheel (garnish)

Turn the page for the recipe!

→

BLUEBERRY SPARKLER

Rum isn't the only liquor that works well in an Italian soda. In fact, there's a good argument to be made that gin is the perfect liquor for that particular format. In any case, the Blueberry Sparkler takes that great gin flavor and complements it with some sweet blueberry simple syrup. A little splash of lemon juice adds some tartness to this drink, which is perfect for sipping on the porch on a hot summer day.

BASIC INGREDIENTS

2 oz. gin

1 oz. blueberry simple syrup

1/2 lemon (juiced)

1 oz. club soda

1 lemon wheel (garnish)

GLASSWARE:
Old Fashioned glass.

1. Add the gin, blueberry simple syrup, and lemon juice to a cocktail shaker filled with ice. Shake vigorously.

2. Strain the resulting mixture into an Old Fashioned glass filled with ice. Top with club soda.

3. Garnish with a lemon wheel.

> WANT TO MAKE FLAVORED SIMPLE SYRUPS? It's easier than it sounds. To infuse your simple syrup with some extra fruit flavor, just add some juice from your fruit of choice during the boiling process. Now you can add a little fruit flavor to your drinks without having to slice anything up!

SNOW BOWL

If gin evokes feelings of Christmas, the Snow Bowl should drive the point home. The flavors in this drink really work overtime to tantalize your taste buds with rich, chocolate, minty goodness. If you're looking for a rich drink that looks as good as it tastes, the Snow Bowl knocks it straight through the uprights. The slight dusting of nutmeg against the white backdrop makes this one drop-dead gorgeous drink.

BASIC INGREDIENTS

 I part gin

 I part white chocolate liqueur

 I splash crème de menthe

 I dusting nutmeg

 GLASSWARE:
Old Fashioned glass.

1. Add the gin, white chocolate liqueur, and crème de menthe to a cocktail shaker filled with ice and shake well.

2. Strain the resulting mixture into an Old Fashioned glass filled with ice.

3. Top with a dusting of nutmeg.

GIN HOT CHOCOLATE

Sticking with the chocolate theme, why not add gin to a familiar winter warmer? If you like hot chocolate, there's no reason you won't love Gin Hot Chocolate as well. This boozy alternative to boring old cocoa even adds a splash of cream liqueur.

BASIC INGREDIENTS

 I part gin

 3 parts hot chocolate

 I part cream liqueur

 I dollop whipped cream

GLASSWARE:

 Irish Coffee glass or a mug.

1. Add gin and hot chocolate to an Irish Coffee glass.

2. Stir in cream liqueur.

3. Top with a dollop of whipped cream.

RUBY FIZZ

The Ruby Fizz is a beautiful and delicious summer cocktail. The fizz of the club soda adds an airiness to this already light cocktail, and the bright red grenadine amplifies the color of the grapefruit juice. It's a simple, elegant cocktail that anyone is sure to love.

BASIC INGREDIENTS

 I part gin

 I part grapefruit juice

 I part club soda

 I splash grenadine

 I grapefruit wedge (garnish)

GLASSWARE:
Highball glass.

1. Add your desired amount of ice to a highball glass and pour in the gin and grapefruit juice. Stir together.

2. Add club soda to fill and stir again. Top with a splash of grenadine for color.

3. Garnish with a grapefruit wedge.

THE BFG

The BFG. The blue freakin' gin drink. It's tasty, it's fresh, and it combines a couple of flavors that don't get combined often enough: gin and grapefruit. The grapefruit also pairs nicely with the slightly bitter sweetness of the Curaçao, allowing this drink to dance across all manner of taste buds. The juniper finish in this drink is a burst of flavor, reminding you it's gin you're drinking.

BASIC INGREDIENTS:

 I part Blue Curaçao

 3 parts Fresca

 I part gin

 GLASSWARE:
Old Fashioned glass.

1. Take an Old Fashioned glass and fill it with ice.

2. Add the gin, followed by the Fresca (or another grapefruit soda of your choice).

3. Top with Blue Curaçao and stir.

BALLAD OF THE SLOTH

What are weekends for? Relaxing—preferably on the couch, and hopefully with a drink in hand. Nothing too taxing on the agenda except some rest and relaxation. Well, the Ballad of the Sloth is the perfect drink for anyone who doesn't want to expend one single ounce of effort. Just gin, club soda, and a little grenadine. Boom, done, a delicious drink that you can happily sip to your heart's content. The simplest of simple cocktails.

BASIC INGREDIENTS:

 1 part gin

 1 part club soda

 1 splash grenadine

 1 maraschino cherry (garnish)

GLASSWARE:
 Old Fashioned glass.

1. Add ice to an Old Fashioned glass and pour in the gin and club soda.

2. Stir thoroughly.

3. Top with grenadine.

4. Garnish with a maraschino cherry.

TEQUILA

Tequila is dangerous, and that's why we love it. Whether you're drinking it in a delicious Margarita or simply sipping it on the rocks, it's hard to deny that there's something magnetic about the strangely earthy taste of tequila.

The adaptability of tequila is part of what makes it truly unique, though. Sometimes it asserts itself; other times, it fades into the background, allowing other flavors to take the lead. What you get out of it depends on how you use it and how deft a hand you have when it comes to complementary flavors.

We start this chapter with Margaritas, of course. But then, while remaining relatively basic, let's be creative and take a deep dive into the flavors that make tequila cocktails great.

CLASSIC MARGARITA

The classic to end all classics. It's not that every Margarita is perfect, but as long as the basic elements are there, chances are you're going to be just fine. The Classic Margarita uses exactly the type of tequila that most of us have lying around the house, with a splash of that traditional orange liqueur to brighten things up. Don't forget to salt the rim!

BASIC INGREDIENTS

 Salt (for rimming)

 2 parts Jose Cuervo Gold tequila

 1 part triple sec

 1 part lime juice

 1 lime slice (garnish)

GLASSWARE:
Margarita glass.

1. Salt the rim of your Margarita glass.

2. Add the tequila, triple sec, and lime juice to a cocktail shaker filled with ice. Shake well.

3. Strain the resulting mixture over ice into your Margarita glass. Garnish with a lime slice.

Many cocktails can be made into a "frozen" version simply by adding a little ice and blending it all together. Frozen Margaritas are a particularly popular option. Just throw a cup or so of ice in the blender with the usual Margarita ingredients, and presto! A perfect frozen treat.

PERFECT MARGARITA

It's not a huge step up from the Classic Margarita, but it is an important one. As seasoned tequila drinkers will tell you, the difference between grabbing the first tequila you see and grabbing a bottle just one shelf higher can be huge. You don't have to break the bank though—try making a Perfect Margarita with Jose Cuervo 1800 Silver tequila instead of your usual Jose Cuervo, and you'll see a huge difference. For a little extra depth of flavor, use Grand Marnier instead of triple sec, too.

BASIC INGREDIENTS

 Salt (for rimming)

 2 parts Jose Cuervo 1800 Silver tequila

 I part Grand Marnier

 I part lime juice

 I lime wheel (garnish)

GLASSWARE:
Margarita glass.

1. Salt the rim of your Margarita glass.

2. Add the tequila, Grand Marnier, and lime juice to a cocktail shaker filled with ice. Shake well.

3. Strain the resulting mixture over ice into your Margarita glass. Garnish with a lime wheel.

There are dozens, hundreds, maybe even thousands of Margarita variations out there. You can use just about any flavor you like, and, as long as you include lime juice and tequila, you can probably still call it a Margarita. Some prefer sugar on the rim of their glass, but salt is traditional.

BUDGET MARGARITA

Bottled margarita mixes are getting tastier as companies perfect their recipes, and there's no reason to turn your nose up at the surprisingly delicious Budget Margarita.

BASIC INGREDIENTS

 Salt (for rimming)

 I part Jose Cuervo Gold tequila

 I part Margarita mix (estimated)

 I lime wedge (garnish)

GLASSWARE:
Margarita glass.

1. Salt the rim of your Margarita glass.

2. Add the tequila and Margarita mix to a cocktail shaker filled with ice. Shake well.

3. Strain the resulting mixture over ice into your Margarita glass. Garnish with a lime wedge.

Different Margarita mixes will sometimes call for different ratios. Read the bottle to check how much you should be using for optimal results. Some will even have specific tequila recommendations, but when in doubt, a mid-level gold tequila will generally work just fine.

VIRGIN MARGARITA

It's hard to replicate the delicious taste of a Margarita. If you're able to accept that the Virgin Margarita is a different cocktail altogether, you'll almost certainly find yourself enjoying this fresh and fruity concoction. Best made with fresh lemon, lime, and orange juice, the Virgin Margarita is the perfect mocktail for morning, afternoon, or night.

BASIC INGREDIENTS

 Salt (for rimming)

 I part lemon juice

 I part lime juice

 I part orange juice

 I part simple syrup

 I lime wedge (garnish)

GLASSWARE:
Margarita glass.

1. Rub the lime along the rim of your Margarita glass and rim it with salt.

2. Add the lemon juice, lime juice, orange juice, and simple syrup to a cocktail shaker filled with ice and shake until combined.

3. Add ice to your Margarita glass and strain the contents of the cocktail shaker into it. Garnish with a lime wedge.

For a Frozen Virgin Margarita, add about a cup of ice (give or take, depending on how thick you want it to be), and blend.

SHOT OF MARG

What if you could pack all of the delicious Margarita flavor into a simple shooter? The Shot of Marg is a resounding response to that question. With the orange and lime flavors playing off the tequila, the Shot of Marg doesn't skimp on taste. It even comes with a familiar salted rim!

BASIC INGREDIENTS

 Salt (for rimming)

 1 oz. tequila

 1/4 oz. triple sec

 1 lime wedge (juiced)

 GLASSWARE:
Shot glass.

1. Rim the edge of a shot glass with salt.

2. Add the tequila and triple sec to the shot glass, then squeeze in the juice from one lime wedge.

3. Lick the salt and then toss back the shot.

COCONUT MARGARITA

You thought we were done with coconut rum when you left the rum section, didn't you? Well think again! Coconut rum isn't just good as the centerpiece of a drink. It's a perfect accent piece as well, as the Coconut Margarita proves. With the soft, understated flavor of coconut providing the perfect bed for the tequila and lime, the Coconut Margarita is sure to become a personal favorite of yours.

BASIC INGREDIENTS

 Coconut shavings (for rimming)

 2 parts tequila

 1 part coconut rum

 1 part lime juice

 1 lime wheel (garnish)

 **GLASSWARE:** Margarita glass.

1. Rim your glass with coconut shavings (use the juice from the lime wheel to make them stick).

2. Add the tequila, coconut rum, and lime juice to a cocktail shaker filled with ice. Shake well.

3. Strain the resulting mixture over ice into your Margarita glass. Garnish with a lime wheel.

CHERRY LIMEADE
MARGARITA

The Cherry Limeade Margarita capitalizes on the lime flavor that is an essential part of any Margarita and substitutes a bit of cherry flavor for the usual orange. The result is even more different than you might expect and makes for an off-kilter treat.

BASIC INGREDIENTS

 Salt (for rimming)

 2 parts tequila

 1 part cherry liqueur

 1 part lime juice

 1 lime wheel (garnish)

 GLASSWARE:
Margarita glass.

1. Salt the rim of your Margarita glass.

2. Add the tequila, cherry liqueur, and lime juice to a cocktail shaker filled with ice. Shake well.

3. Strain the resulting mixture over ice into your Margarita glass. Garnish with a lime wheel.

TEQUILA SUNRISE

1 part tequila

1 dash lemon juice

2 parts orange juice

1 splash grenadine

1 maraschino cherry (garnish)

1 orange slice (garnish)

Turn the page for the recipe!

⟶

TEQUILA SUNRISE

The (maybe) more popular sister of the Vodka Sunrise, the Tequila Sunrise makes use of the same vivid coloration to present a drink that is both delicious and beautiful to behold. Combining the ever-popular flavors of tequila and orange juice, along with an accent of grenadine, the Tequila Sunrise is a drink that absolutely lives up to the billing.

BASIC INGREDIENTS

 1 part tequila

 1 dash lemon juice

 2 parts orange juice

 1 splash grenadine

 1 maraschino cherry (garnish)

1 orange slice (garnish)

 GLASSWARE: Highball glass.

1. Add ice to a highball glass and pour in the tequila and a dash of lemon juice. Mix together.

2. Add orange juice to fill, then top with a splash of grenadine. Don't stir the drink. Instead allow the grenadine to slowly filter down through the orange juice and tequila.

3. Garnish with a maraschino cherry and an orange slice.

VARIATION

If this sounds enticing but you're fresh out of tequila, go back to the Vodka Sunrise (page 60).

VIRGIN SUNRISE

Drinks bearing the "sunrise" name are a rare breed in that they tend to be as delicious as they are beautiful. The Virgin Sunrise makes the argument that you don't need booze to create a perfectly acceptable (and naturally delicious) variant. The Virgin Sunrise is as easy to make as adding a splash of grenadine to your orange juice, but the subtle flavor it adds and gorgeous color it creates make this a mocktail worth trying.

BASIC INGREDIENTS

 1 glass orange juice

 1 splash grenadine

 1 orange wheel (garnish)

 GLASSWARE:
Hurricane glass.

1. Add orange juice to a glass filled with ice.

2. Top with a splash of grenadine.

3. Garnish with an orange wheel.

DARK WINGS

Similar to the popular El Diablo cocktail, the Dark Wings drink couples tequila with a dark liqueur to create a medley of surprisingly light flavors. The bite of the ginger beer pairs well with tequila, and the blackberry liqueur and lime add sweet and sour elements to the drink.

BASIC INGREDIENTS

I part silver tequila

I part blackberry liqueur

I lime (juiced)

2 parts ginger beer

I handful blackberries (garnish)

GLASSWARE:
Highball glass.

1. Add the tequila, blackberry liqueur, and lime juice to a cocktail shaker filled with ice. Shake well.

2. Strain the resulting mixture into a highball glass filled with ice. Top with ginger beer.

3. Garnish with a handful of blackberries.

VARIATION

If you don't have blackberries on hand, other garnish options include a lime wedge, a cherry, or a slice of kiwi—or all three.

PALOMA PLUS

The simple paloma is a mix of complementary flavors: one part tequila, three parts grapefruit soda. But why stop there when there are so many other flavors that accent these so well? A splash of grapefruit juice can elevate the grapefruit soda, and a bit of fresh lime juice is a plus in just about any cocktail.

BASIC INGREDIENTS

 I part tequila

 I splash grapefruit juice

 I lime wedge (juiced)

 2 parts Fresca (grapefruit soda)

 I grapefruit wedge (garnish)

 GLASSWARE: Highball glass.

1. Add the tequila, grapefruit juice, and lime juice to a highball glass filled with ice. Mix together.

2. Top with Fresca and stir again. Garnish with a grapefruit wedge.

TEQUILA GRAPEFRUIT COCKTAIL

Tequila and orange are an essential part of any Margarita, but they don't need to be tied down by tradition. The Tequila Grapefruit Cocktail adds a healthy dose of a different citrus fruit, and it is an extremely welcome addition to this fresh, fruity drink. This cocktail is refreshing any time of year and a go-to morning drink for those looking for an a.m. treat.

BASIC INGREDIENTS

 I part gold tequila

 I part ginger ale

 2 parts grapefruit juice

 I dash orange liqueur

 I grapefruit slice (garnish)

 I maraschino cherry (garnish)

 GLASSWARE:
Highball glass.

1. Add ice to a highball glass, then add the the tequila, ginger ale, grapefruit juice, and orange liqueur.

2. Stir until thoroughly mixed.

3. Garnish with a grapefruit slice and a cherry.

VARATION

If you don't have a grapefruit slice available, an orange slice will do.

MEXICAN MULE

Like the Moscow Mule (or the Mint Mule, see page 32), the Mexican Mule takes advantage of the distinctive tastes of lime and ginger beer to craft a memorable and delicious cocktail. Whereas the Mint Mule put a fresh spin on a classic recipe, the splash of triple sec in the Mexican Mule begs you to remember your last Margarita.

BASIC INGREDIENTS

 I part tequila

 I splash triple sec

 I lime wedge (juiced)

 2 parts ginger beer

 I lime wheel (garnish)

GLASSWARE:
Highball glass
(or copper mug).

1. Pour the tequila and triple sec into a glass filled with ice, then squeeze in the juice from one lime wedge.

2. Top with ginger beer and stir until thoroughly mixed.

3. Garnish with a lime wheel.

BAJA LEMONADE

1 sprig rosemary

1 part tequila

1 splash coconut rum

2 parts lemonade

1 lemon wheel (garnish)

Turn the page for the recipe!

BAJA LEMONADE

Yes, more coconut rum! And why not, when you want to evoke a sense of the tropics? Baja Lemonade is more than just a simple tequila and lemonade concoction, adding a bit of coconut and rosemary to ensure that the flavor transcends the simplicity. Maybe a standard tequila and lemonade is more your speed, but if you're looking for something a little bit out there, Baja Lemonade is the drink for you.

BASIC INGREDIENTS

 I sprig rosemary

 I part tequila

 I splash coconut rum

 2 parts lemonade

I lemon wheel (garnish)

GLASSWARE:
Highball glass.

1. Add the rosemary, tequila, and coconut rum to a cocktail shaker filled with ice. Shake vigorously.

2. Strain the mixture into a highball glass filled with ice. Top with lemonade.

3. Garnish with a lemon wheel.

VIRGIN BAJA LEMONADE

The coconut flavor is a big part of what makes the Baja Lemonade such a delicious treat, and there's no reason you can't remove the tequila and capture that same delicious flavor profile. Instead, simply add a bit of agave syrup as a sweetener, and go with coconut syrup rather than coconut rum. The result is a tasty treat for a summer's day, a drink that is miles away from regular old lemonade.

BASIC INGREDIENTS

 5 parts lemonade

 1 part coconut syrup

 1 splash agave syrup

 1 sprig rosemary

 1 lemon wheel (garnish)

GLASSWARE:
Highball glass.

1. Fill a cocktail shaker with ice, the liquid ingredients, and rosemary. Shake well.

2. Strain the resulting mixture into a highball glass filled with ice.

3. Garnish with a lemon wheel.

CANCUN COFFEE

Irish Coffee. Cuban Coffee. Why not Cancun Coffee? The rounded flavor of the tequila pairs surprisingly well with coffee—a bolder man than I might even say better than whiskey does. A bit of coffee and cream liqueur complete this delicious treat. Need a boost to keep you going but don't want to sacrifice your buzz? Cancun Coffee is the way to go.

BASIC INGREDIENTS

 1 part tequila

 1 part coffee liqueur

 2 parts coffee

 1 splash cream liqueur

 GLASSWARE:
Irish Coffee glass or a mug.

1. Add tequila and coffee liqueur to an Irish Coffee glass. Top with coffee.

2. Finish with a splash of cream liqueur and stir until thoroughly mixed.

230

EARLY NIGHT

The Early Night is a drink so delicious that you might forget how strong it is. In fact, it's so deceptively potent that just a few might end your night before it even begins, hence its name. But if you can handle your alcohol and you're after flavor, you could do worse than starting your night with one or two of these.

BASIC INGREDIENTS

 I part tequila

 I part cherry liqueur

 1/2 lime (juiced)

 2 parts orange juice

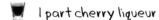 I slice starfruit (garnish)

 I maraschino cherry (garnish)

 GLASSWARE: Highball glass.

1. Add the tequila and cherry liqueur to your highball glass filled with ice. Squeeze in the juice from ½ of a lime.

2. Top with orange juice and stir until thoroughly mixed. Garnish with a slice of starfruit and a cherry.

VARIATIONS

■ If cherry isn't your favorite flavor, feel free to mix in a different type of liqueur. Melon liqueur and limoncello work almost as well, or you can choose your favorite.

■ If starfruit is too fancy for you, an orange wheel does the trick.

END OF THE LIME

Tequila and lime is a combination seemingly as old as liquor itself, and the reason should be obvious. There are few flavor combinations that enjoy such consistent success in the cocktail world, and whether you're taking shots or mixing cocktails, these two ingredients are never far from each other. Try mixing some tequila into a little lemon-lime soda, and add some fresh lime juice to really bring out the flavor!

BASIC INGREDIENTS

 I part tequila

 1/2 lime (juiced)

 2 parts Sprite
(or lemon-lime soda)

 I lime wedge (garnish)

 GLASSWARE:
Highball glass.

1. Pour the tequila over ice and add the lime juice. Top with Sprite.

2. Garnish with a lime wedge.

BLOODY MARIA EXPRESS

As with the Bloody Mary, the Bloody Maria Express is a traditional morning cocktail that can help you kick any hangover. Trimmed down a bit from the standard Bloody Maria, which tends to be overflowing with ingredients, the Bloody Maria Express reduces the drink to its essentials. After all, the real joy of any Bloody Mary variation lies in the absurd garnishes. Be creative!

BASIC INGREDIENTS

 I dash Worcestershire sauce

 I dash lemon juice

 I part tequila

 2 parts tomato juice

 Anything your heart desires (garnish)

 GLASSWARE:
Pint glass.

1. Add the Worcestershire sauce and lemon juice to a pint glass, then add ice.

2. Pour in the tequila and tomato juice and stir until thoroughly mixed.

3. Garnish with anything you want— lemon, lime, cilantro, olives, or even bacon.

BERRY BURSTER

1 Kiwi (sliced)

4 strawberries (sliced)

1 part tequila

1 part strawberry Kiwi juice

Turn the page for the recipe!

BERRY BURSTER

When it comes to fresh fruit, why stop at just the juice? Sure, lime juice, lemon juice, apple juice, and other fresh fruit juices can be extremely useful and flavorful additions to a cocktail. But sometimes, adding the fruit itself can take a drink to the next level. Of course, the best part of adding fresh fruit to a cocktail is that when you're done, you've got a delicious treat that's been soaking up all that boozy goodness.

BASIC INGREDIENTS

 1 Kiwi (sliced)

 4 strawberries (sliced)

 1 part tequila

 1 part strawberry Kiwi juice

 GLASSWARE:
Old Fashioned glass.

1. Peel and slice the kiwi, then hull and slice the strawberries. Save a slice of kiwi as a garnish, then muddle together the rest of the sliced fruit in the bottom of an Old Fashioned glass.

2. Add ice to the glass, then add the tequila and strawberry kiwi juice.

3. Garnish with a slice of kiwi. Don't forget to eat the booze-infused fruit when you finish!

> **PATIENCE IS A VIRTUE.** If you're making a drink that involves slices of fruit or other edible ingredients, you might consider sealing it up and leaving it in the fridge overnight. Not only will it ensure that you have a crisp, cool beverage the next day, but it will give the drink extra time to soak into the fruit!

APPLE TART

Why do so many tequila drinks feature sweet and sour flavors like apple and lime? Because they just work so well together. The Apple Tart features the pucker-worthy sourness of apple schnapps and lime juice, tempered with a little bit of sweet apple juice. Similar in flavor and color to the ever-popular Appletini, the Apple Tart is an off-the-beaten-path tequila drink for anytime.

BASIC INGREDIENTS

2 parts tequila

1 part apple schnapps

1 part apple juice

1 lime (juiced)

GLASSWARE:
Highball glass.

1. Add the ingredients to a cocktail shaker filled with ice. Shake vigorously.

2. Fill a highball glass with ice and strain the tequila mixture into it.

VARIATION

Any apple juice will do for the Apple Tart, but if you have access to fresh apple juice or can juice it yourself, you may find the added freshness well worth it.

TEQUILA SPARKLER

If you like a little carbonation with your tequila cocktails but aren't interested in going the easy route with cola or ginger ale, the Tequila Sparkler might be for you. Integrating the bubbly sweetness of champagne will leave you feeling fresh, especially after you squeeze in a little bit of that fresh lime juice familiar to so many tequila cocktail recipes. It's the perfect cocktail for a New Year's Eve party or other festive celebration!

BASIC INGREDIENTS

1 part tequila

1 splash lime juice

3 parts champagne

1 lime wedge (garnish)

GLASSWARE:
Champagne flute.

1. Pour tequila and lime juice into a champagne flute. Top with champagne.

2. Garnish with a lime wedge.

TEQUILA LIME SODA

Simple, like an Italian soda, and just as delicious. Some drinks really benefit from that extra fizz, and the Tequila Lime Soda is one of them. With a light feel and the same great flavor you've come to expect from a tequila and lime concoction, this is a drink that proves less can be more.

BASIC INGREDIENTS

1 part silver tequila

1 part lime juice

3 parts club soda

1 lime wheel (garnish)

GLASSWARE:
Old Fashioned glass.

1. Pour the tequila and lime into an Old Fashioned glass filled with ice. Stir lightly.

2. Top with club soda.

3. Garnish with a lime wheel.

UNLIKELY ALLIES

Tequila and champagne! They go together like...well, like two delicious things that you don't see together very often. This is a shame, because the muted, round flavor of tequila combines with the dry sharpness of champagne in an unexpectedly delightful way. Bind the two flavors together with a hit of grapefruit soda and you've got a unique cocktail that everyone will want to try.

BASIC INGREDIENTS:

1 part tequila

1 part grapefruit soda

2 parts champagne

GLASSWARE:
Champagne flute.

1. Add tequila to a champagne flute.

2. Pour in the grapefruit soda and lightly swirl the glass to stir.

3. Top with champagne.

TEQUILA CIDER

Tequila and apple go together better than you might think. In fact, some of you may even have had tequila-barrel aged hard cider by now—so you know it's delicious. This particular drink is a boozy concoction that blends a nice, dry hard cider with that most dangerous of liquors, plus a nice splash of regular apple cider to give it a little extra backbone. Enjoy!

BASIC INGREDIENTS

 I part tequila

 4 parts dry hard cider

 I part apple cider

 GLASSWARE:
Old Fashioned glass.

1. Add ice to an Old Fashioned glass, then pour in the tequila, hard cider, and cider.

2. Stir until thoroughly mixed.

TEQUILA SPRITZER

Tequila, grapefruit, and lime are three flavors that go together, so why overthink things? This quick and easy cocktail is perfect for an evening in, an evening out, or any anything in between. It's crisp and refreshing, and a great accompaniment for brunch or dinner.

BASIC INGREDIENTS:

1 part tequila

3 parts grapefruit juice

1 part club soda
(or grapefruit seltzer)

1 splash lime juice

1 lime wheel (garnish)

GLASSWARE:
Pint glass.

1. Add the tequila, grapefruit juice, club soda, and lime juice to a pint glass filled with ice.

2. Stir thoroughly.

3. Garnish with a lime wheel.

TEQUILA MOJITO

Why let rum have all the fun? Most flavors that work well with rum also work well with tequila, and with that in mind there's no reason you can't adapt that most classic of rum cocktails to work with the tequila gathering dust in your liquor cabinet. This is a minty, lime-tastic treat that you'll be shocked you never thought of before.

BASIC INGREDIENTS:

 I part tequila

 2 parts lime seltzer

 I splash simple syrup

 6 mint leaves

 I lime wheel (garnish)

 GLASSWARE:
Highball glass.

1. Muddle the mint leaves and simple syrup in the bottom of a highball glass, then add ice.

2. Add the tequila and seltzer.

3. Stir until thoroughly mixed.

4. Garnish with a lime wheel.

MEXICAN CHOCOLATE

Whether we're talking about Mexican chocolate cake or a simple mole sauce, there's just something about chocolate that agrees with the flavors of Mexico. It turns out that tequila is no exception, as a little chocolate liqueur and cream elevate the spirit's flavor into something greater.

BASIC INGREDIENTS:

1 part silver tequila

1 part chocolate liqueur

1 part milk or cream

1 dusting cocoa powder (garnish)

GLASSWARE:
Cocktail glass.

1. Add tequila, chocolate liqueur, and milk or cream to a cocktail shaker filled with ice.

2. Shake vigorously.

3. Strain the resulting mixture into a cocktail glass.

4. Garnish with a dusting of cocoa powder.

CACTUS BLOOM

Tequila goes great with a wide range of different flavors, but people often give in to the temptation to simply make a new Margarita variant. While this book does include a number of Margarita recipes, it's important to remember that tequila and cranberry don't need to form a Cranberry Margarita to be delicious. The Cactus Bloom takes precisely those two flavors and gives them a minty fresh twist for a cocktail that feels both new and familiar.

BASIC INGREDIENTS:

 6 mint leaves

 I part silver tequila

 4 parts cranberry juice

 I dash lime juice

 Sugar (for rimming)

 I lime wedge (garnish)

 GLASSWARE:
Highball glass.

1. Tear the mint leaves in half and add them to a cocktail shaker filled with ice.

2. Add the tequila, cranberry juice, and lime juice to the cocktail shaker.

3. Shake vigorously.

4. Wet the edge of a highball glass and rim it with sugar.

5. Fill the glass with ice. Strain the contents of the cocktail shaker into the highball glass.

6. Garnish with a lime wedge.

SILVERBLOOD

Vermouth is one of those spirits that you should always have in your liquor cabinet. It goes well with many different liquors, though you rarely see it with tequila. The Silverblood cocktail looks to change that, adding a hit of sweet vermouth to silver tequila, and adding layers of orange liqueur and grenadine to give it a complete, well-rounded flavor profile. You might not have thought to mix these ingredients together, but you're sure to love it.

BASIC INGREDIENTS:

 3 parts silver tequila

 1 part sweet vermouth

 1 part triple sec

 1 splash grenadine

GLASSWARE:
Cocktail glass.

1. Add the tequila, vermouth, triple sec, and grenadine to a cocktail shaker filled with ice.

2. Shake vigorously.

3. Strain the resulting mixture into a cocktail glass.

> Some drinks specifically recommend silver tequila as opposed to gold tequila. Most of the time, this recommendation is less about flavor and more about the color of the drink. If you don't mind muddling the colors and prefer the flavor of gold tequila to silver, feel free to use any tequila you like.

WHISKEY

A traditional Irish folk song says, "Whiskey you're the devil." But that couldn't be more wrong. In any of its forms, whiskey is a delight. Whether it's the peaty smokiness of a well-aged scotch, the caramel sweetness of bourbon, or the spicy, full-bodied taste of a nice rye, whiskey has something to offer a wide variety of different cocktails. And as any whiskey enthusiast will tell you, consuming the delicious beverage on its own is also a treat.

The beauty of whiskey of any kind is that it lends itself well to simple cocktails. Those who enjoy whiskey enjoy its taste, and so it should come as no surprise that whiskey cocktails tend to promote the taste of the whiskey rather than drown it out, a la vodka. Common ingredients are accents such as simple syrup, maraschino cherries, sweet vermouth, and other more subtle flavors that don't run the risk of overwhelming the whiskey.

Whiskey cocktails tend to best serve the whiskey lover. If you don't consider yourself a fan of the dark liquor, chances are these cocktails aren't for you. But if you're a whiskey enthusiast, you may find yourself unable to stop drinking these delicious concoctions. Come to think of it, maybe the song is right.

CLASSIC OLD FASHIONED

It's hard to anoint a "favorite" whiskey cocktail, but the Old Fashioned certainly challenges for the spot. Featuring just simple syrup, bitters, and a little bit of citrus to accent the flavor of the whiskey, the Old Fashioned is a sophisticated drink for the seasoned whiskey drinker. For the classic version of the cocktail, an underrated, extremely drinkable whiskey like Maker's Mark is perfect.

BASIC INGREDIENTS

 I splash simple syrup

 I strip orange peel

 2 drops bitters

 2 oz. Maker's Mark bourbon whiskey

 I maraschino cherry (garnish)

 GLASSWARE:
Old Fashioned glass.

1. Add the simple syrup to an Old Fashioned glass and drop in a strip of orange peel. Add the bitters and muddle together.

2. Fill the glass with ice, then add your bourbon. Stir together slowly.

3. Garnish with a maraschino cherry.

VARIATION

Some versions of the Old Fashioned call for the inclusion of club soda to give the drink a bit of fizz. This isn't traditionally included, but as always, it's up to you.

PERFECT
OLD FASHIONED

For the Perfect Old Fashioned, eschew the simple syrup in favor of a sugar cube and some water, and rely on the orange slice garnish for the small punch of citrus that the drink requires. Using a top-shelf whiskey like Woodford Reserve will enhance the drinkability of the cocktail, while still keeping you in a reasonable price range. Sure, you could spend hundreds of dollars on bourbon. But if you do that, you probably aren't watering it down in a cocktail, no matter how delicious it may be.

BASIC INGREDIENTS

I sugar cube

2 drops bitters

I splash water

2 oz. Woodford Reserve bourbon whiskey

I orange slice (garnish)

I maraschino cherry (garnish)

GLASSWARE:
Old Fashioned glass.

1. Add the sugar cube to your glass. Saturate with bitters. Add a small splash of water and muddle.

2. Fill the glass with ice and add the bourbon. Stir lightly. Garnish with a slice of orange and a maraschino cherry.

BUDGET OLD FASHIONED

On the other hand, why go all out when there are plenty of perfectly affordable whiskeys that will do just fine? Take Evan Williams bourbon whiskey, for example. A decent-tasting, budget-friendly alternative to expensive options like Woodford Reserve and Maker's Mark. When you're craving a cocktail, you're not necessarily craving the best, most expensive ingredients. You're craving a way to scratch that itch, and the Budget Old Fashioned will do the job just fine.

BASIC INGREDIENTS

 I splash simple syrup

 2 drops bitters

 I maraschino cherry

 2 oz. Evan Williams bourbon whiskey

 GLASSWARE: Old Fashioned glass.

1. Add the simple syrup, bitters, and maraschino cherry to your glass. Muddle together.

2. Fill the glass with ice. Add bourbon and stir lightly.

COFFEE OLD FASHIONED

Irish Coffee (page 294) is a beloved drink, but coffee works well with other whiskey drinks, too. In this cocktail, coffee takes the place of vermouth in a classic Old Fashioned, creating a slightly bitter, slightly sweet alternative cocktail that is bursting with creativity!

BASIC INGREDIENTS:

 I part whiskey

 2 parts coffee (hot or iced)

 I splash simple syrup

 I dash bitters

 I pinch coffee beans (garnish)

 GLASSWARE:
Old Fashioned glass.

1. Add simple syrup and bitters to an Old Fashioned Glass.

2. If using iced coffee, add ice.

3. Add whiskey and coffee.

4. Stir thoroughly.

5. Top with a few coffee beans.

> You probably don't want to eat the unroasted coffee beans here...but you can always sub in chocolate-covered coffee beans or another similarly tasty edible version.

WHISKEY SOUR

Ah yes, the famous Whiskey Sour. Made a variety of different ways, sometimes with egg whites, sometimes with sour mix, and sometimes simply with lemon juice. The drink is as sour as its name implies, adding an unexpected new dimension to the whiskey. Smashing whiskey and lemon juice together head-on, this delicious, classic concoction is what comes out of the wreckage.

BASIC INGREDIENTS

 2 1/2 oz. rye whiskey

 1 oz. lemon juice

 1/3 oz. simple syrup

 1 maraschino cherry (garnish)

 1 orange slice (garnish)

 GLASSWARE:
Old Fashioned glass.

1. Add the whiskey, lemon juice, and simple syrup to a cocktail shaker filled with ice. Shake vigorously.

2. Strain the resulting mixture into an Old Fashioned glass filled with ice.

3. Garnish with a maraschino cherry and a slice of orange.

BUDGET SOUR

One of the great things about living in the modern age is convenience. There are microwave dinners, there are smartphones, and anyone who doesn't feel like mixing a cocktail can go out and buy a mix to make their lives easier. As far as mixes go, sour mix is probably one of the more popular options and makes the Budget Sour a convenient, hassle-free alternative to the traditional Whiskey Sour.

BASIC INGREDIENTS

 1 part rye whiskey

 2 parts sour mix

 1 lemon slice

 GLASSWARE:
Old Fashioned glass.

1. Add the whiskey and sour mix to an Old Fashioned glass filled with ice. Stir until thoroughly mixed.

2. Garnish with a lemon slice.

Different mixes from different companies may recommend mixing in different proportions. Be sure to read the label on the packaging to know for sure, but 2:1 is usually a good ratio.

CLASSIC
MANHATTAN

2 oz. Knob Creek rye whiskey

2/3 oz. sweet vermouth

2 drops bitters

Cherries (garnish)

Turn the page for the recipe!

→

CLASSIC MANHATTAN

Whiskey and vermouth is a classic combination, and one it's difficult to go wrong with. The Manhattan makes use of this simple combination and, with the addition of just a few drops of bitters, creates something truly fantastic. A refined and elegant cocktail, the Classic Manhattan offers the everyday mixologist a simple way to enjoy an old classic.

BASIC INGREDIENTS

 2 oz. Knob Creek rye whiskey

 2/3 oz. sweet vermouth

 2 drops bitters

 Cherries (garnish)

 GLASSWARE: Cocktail glass.

1. Fill a mixing glass with ice and add the liquid ingredients. Stir gently to avoid bruising the drink.

2. Strain the resulting mixture into a cocktail glass.

3. Garnish with a cherry or two.

If you've ever heard someone talk about not wanting to "bruise" their drink, you might have wondered what they meant. A bruised drink contains more water than it should, which can leave it with a muddy appearance. Usually this is in reference to whiskey, but gin also gets this designation. Bruising usually occurs when a cocktail is shaken.

PERFECT MANHATTAN

When it comes to a cocktail as classy as the Manhattan, why settle for anything less than the finest ingredients? By building your drink around top-shelf whiskey, you can be sure that you're getting the best tasting Manhattan around. The Perfect Manhattan is made using WhistlePig Straight Rye, one of the most delicious whiskeys the average person can get their hands on.

BASIC INGREDIENTS

 2 oz. WhistlePig Straight Rye

 2/3 oz. sweet vermouth

 2 drops bitters

 1 maraschino cherry (garnish)

 GLASSWARE: Cocktail glass.

1. Fill a mixing glass with ice and add the liquid ingredients. Stir gently to avoid bruising the drink.

2. Put a maraschino cherry in the bottom of a cocktail glass and strain the contents of the mixing glass over it.

BUDGET MANHATTAN

One of the great things about the Manhattan is its adaptability. While tradition dictates that it be made with rye whiskey, contemporary mixologists have begun to use bourbon with increasing regularity. And chances are, you're more likely to have some affordable bourbon lying around than you are rye whiskey. So why not make a Budget Manhattan? It might not be by the book (although if you're following these instructions, it technically is now), but it still packs a punch, as well as a rich, delicious flavor.

BASIC INGREDIENTS

 2 oz. Jim Beam bourbon

 2/3 oz. sweet vermouth

 2 drops bitters

 1 maraschino cherry (garnish)

 GLASSWARE:
Old Fashioned glass.

1. Fill a mixing glass with ice and add the bourbon, vermouth, and bitters. Stir gently to avoid bruising the drink.

2. Strain the mixture into an Old Fashioned glass. Garnish with a cherry.

ROB ROY

2 oz. scotch whiskey

1 oz. sweet vermouth

2 drops bitters

1 maraschino cherry (garnish)

Turn the page for the recipe!

→

ROB ROY

The Rob Roy is, essentially, a Manhattan for those who prefer scotch. Made with simply whiskey, vermouth, and bitters, the Rob Roy swaps out rye whiskey (or bourbon) in favor of scotch's smoky flavor. The Rob Roy hasn't attained quite the same level of popularity as its rye-based contemporary, but it is no less delicious. As with many cocktails, your stance on the matter comes down to personal preference.

BASIC INGREDIENTS

 2 oz. scotch whiskey

 1 oz. sweet vermouth

 2 drops bitters

 1 maraschino cherry (garnish)

 GLASSWARE:
Cocktail glass.

1. Fill a mixing glass with ice and add the liquid ingredients. Stir gently to avoid bruising the drink.

2. Add a maraschino cherry to your cocktail glass and strain the contents of the mixing glass over it.

CLASSIC MINT JULEP

Who doesn't love a mint julep? The classic drink of the Kentucky Derby, the mint julep has remained popular with whiskey drinkers for over 100 years. With a mid-range, drinkable bourbon and a little powdered sugar (the powdered sugar is important if you want to do it right), this is a cocktail sure to see many new converts after just one taste.

BASIC INGREDIENTS

 4 mint leaves

 1 tsp. powdered sugar

 1 splash water

 2 oz. Maker's Mark bourbon whiskey

 1 mint sprig (garnish)

 GLASSWARE:
Old Fashioned glass.

1. Tear the mint leaves in half to release their flavor, then muddle in the bottom of your glass with powdered sugar and water.

2. Fill the glass with cracked ice, then add the bourbon. Stir gently.

3. Garnish with a sprig of mint.

PERFECT MINT JULEP

Why not take the mint julep to a bit more high-end place? If you truly appreciate subtle flavor and nuance (and are willing to spend a bit extra on the best bourbon), you can make your mint julep a truly transcendent drinking experience. Be sure you drink it out of a silver or pewter cup—if you're going to call something "perfect," you'd better go all the way. The Perfect Mint Julep does just that.

BASIC INGREDIENTS

 4 mint leaves

 1 tsp. powdered sugar

 1 splash water

 2 oz. Woodford Reserve bourbon whiskey

 1 mint sprig (garnish)

 GLASSWARE:
Silver or pewter cup.

1. Muddle the mint leaves in the bottom of the cup with powdered sugar and water.

2. Fill the cup with cracked ice, then add your bourbon. Stir until the outside of your cup is visibly chilled.

3. Garnish with a sprig of mint.

BUDGET MINT JULEP

So you want a mint julep, but you don't have the ingredients to do it exactly as described. No matter. There is a way to make a perfectly acceptable mint julep with whatever you have on hand. The beauty of the mint julep is that while it has a reputation for being a refined cocktail, the ingredients are simple enough that just about anyone can make it (as long as you've got some mint on hand!).

BASIC INGREDIENTS

 4 mint leaves

 1 tsp. sugar

 1 splash water

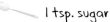 2 oz. Evan Williams bourbon whiskey

 1 mint sprig (garnish)

GLASSWARE:
Highball glass.

1. Never mind the powdered sugar; regular sugar will work just fine. Muddle the sugar in your glass with the water and mint leaves (tear them in half to release additional flavor).

2. Fill the glass with ice, then add your bourbon. Stir gently.

3. Garnish with a sprig of mint.

WHALEN SMASH

Whiskey and ginger is a time-honored flavor combination, but precious few whiskey cocktails include mint. The Whalen Smash forgoes the ginger liqueurs that similar cocktails call for, instead adding a splash of ginger ale to give the drink some added lightness. The carbonation gives the drink a playful element, but doesn't overwhelm the palate, leaving plenty of room for the mint and lemon to play off one another.

BASIC INGREDIENTS

 1/2 lemon, cut into thirds

 4 mint leaves

 3 parts bourbon whiskey

 1 part ginger beer

GLASSWARE:
Old Fashioned glass.

1. Squeeze the lemon wedges into your glass. Drop the squeezed wedges into the glass.

2. Add the mint to the glass and muddle with the lemon juice. Add ice as desired.

3. Pour in the bourbon, then top with ginger beer. Stir together.

VARIATION

A slice of lime is always welcome.

CINNAMON
APPLE

2 parts apple cider

1 part apple liqueur

1 part cinnamon whiskey

1 cinnamon stick (garnish)

Turn the page for the recipe!

→

CINNAMON APPLE

Whether in an apple pie or an apple crumble, there are few flavors that go together more perfectly than cinnamon and apple. It might even be called the quintessential flavor of our land—after all, what's more American than apple pie? But pies are work, and they take time. Why spend the whole day preparing an apple pie when you can *drink* one instead? The Cinnamon Apple cocktail features the delicious flavors you expect from your favorite homemade treat, but with a delightful buzz in lieu of the sugar rush.

BASIC INGREDIENTS

 2 parts apple cider

 1 part apple liqueur

 1 part cinnamon whiskey

 1 cinnamon stick (garnish)

 GLASSWARE:
Old Fashioned glass.

1. Fill an Old Fashioned glass with ice and add the cider, apple liqueur, and cinnamon whiskey. Stir until thoroughly mixed.

2. Garnish with a cinnamon stick.

VARIATIONS

- To soften the flavor a bit, add a bit of amaretto or even some orgeat syrup.
- If the tartness of the apple liqueur is overwhelming, you can omit it in favor of just cider and whiskey.

VIRGIN
CINNAMON APPLE

Cinnamon and apple are a celebrated flavor combination that extends well beyond alcoholic beverages. Here, sparkling cider, cinnamon, and a cinnamon stick transform apple cider into a delicious fall mocktail.

BASIC INGREDIENTS

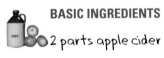 2 parts apple cider

 1 part sparkling cider

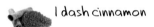 1 dash cinnamon

 1 cinnamon stick (garnish)

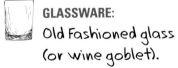 **GLASSWARE:**
Old Fashioned glass (or wine goblet).

1. Fill a glass with ice and add the ciders and cinnamon. Stir until mixed.

2. Garnish with a cinnamon stick.

MISH MASH

Ever forget to restock your liquor cabinet for a few weeks, or maybe even months? Once in a while, you open the cabinet and realize you're left with just a handful of odds and ends. The Mish Mash takes a couple of things that you should always have around a half bottle of, mixes in a bit of bourbon, and gives you a surprisingly delicious result.

BASIC INGREDIENTS

 2 parts bourbon whiskey

 1 part triple sec

 1 part simple syrup

 1 splash grenadine

 GLASSWARE:
Old Fashioned glass.

1. Fill a glass with ice and add bourbon, triple sec, and simple syrup.

2. Stir together until mixed. Top with a splash of grenadine.

VARIATION

Feel free to swap out the triple sec for a different type of liqueur, such as raspberry, strawberry, or lemon.

IRISH ROSE

With its rosy color, the Irish Rose is an attractive alternative to the more common whiskey cocktails. The unusual combination of whiskey and Sprite works surprisingly well, especially with the subtle flavor of grenadine bridging the gap.

BASIC INGREDIENTS

 2 parts Irish whiskey

 3 parts Sprite

 1 part grenadine

 1 lemon wedge (garnish)

 GLASSWARE: Old Fashioned glass.

1. Add ice to your glass, then add in the whiskey and Sprite.

2. Top with a splash of grenadine and stir together until a rosy color is achieved.

3. Garnish with a wedge of lemon.

The great thing about most cocktails is that they're so easy to tweak to fit your purposes. If you have a favorite cocktail but don't have all of the ingredients, it can be a rewarding experience to play around and see if you can use what you have to create something just as tasty!

IRISH COFFEE

The perfect wake-up cocktail and a favorite of airport bar patrons (or maybe that's just me). Irish Coffee is made a variety of ways, with some including Irish cream, some not, some specifying Irish whiskey, some not. But it just doesn't feel like "Irish" Coffee without Jameson and Baileys, does it?

BASIC INGREDIENTS

 3 parts coffee

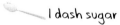 1 dash sugar

 1 part Jameson Irish whiskey

 1 part Baileys Irish Cream

 Whipped cream (garnish)

 GLASSWARE:
Irish Coffee glass or a mug.

1. Pour the coffee into your glass or mug and add sugar. Stir until the sugar has dissolved.

2. Add whiskey and stir again.

3. Top with Baileys Irish Cream. If you can, layer the cream on top rather than stirring it in.

4. If desired, garnish with a dollop of whipped cream.

BOURBON SWEET TEA

Bourbon is a favorite drink of the South, and so is sweet tea. What could be more natural than mixing them together to create a refreshing and delicious beverage perfect for beating the heat? It's the ideal spur-of-the-moment drink, devoid of fancy ingredients or complicated instructions. Just mix your tea and bourbon with a little bit of lemon and enjoy! *Makes 4 servings.*

BASIC INGREDIENTS

 1/2 lemon (juiced)

 1 part bourbon

 4 parts sweet tea

 4 lemon wheels (garnish)

GLASSWARE:
Pint glass.

1. Squeeze the juice from ½ of a lemon into a pitcher. Add the juiced portion to the pitcher.

2. Add ice, then pour in the bourbon and sweet tea. Stir until thoroughly mixed.

3. Pour into individual glasses and garnish each with a lemon wheel.

VARIATION

Sweet tea too overwhelming for you? You can always make this drink with unsweetened, fresh-brewed iced tea.

Store-bought iced teas and lemonades work just fine, but if you're feeling particularly industrious you might want to make your own. Play around with the proportion of lemon and sugar until you find a lemonade mixture you're happy with, or throw a bunch of your favorite tea bags into some boiling water and let them brew for a while. It might be harder than just pouring it out of a bottle, but you'll be surprised at how much better it will taste!

MASH EFFECT

What is sour mash? Excellent question! You've probably seen it on the side of some whiskey bottles. It's similar to sourdough bread: the fermentation of sour mash whiskey uses material from an older, existing mash. So if you ever thought twice about buying sour mash whiskey because you were afraid it might have a sour flavor, never fear — that's not what it refers to. Now that you've learned a little something, here's a fun drink!

BASIC INGREDIENTS:

 2 parts sour mash whiskey

 1 part sweet vermouth

 1 part cherry cola

 1 maraschino cherry (garnish)

 GLASSWARE:
Old Fashioned glass.

1. Add ice to an Old Fashioned glass. Pour in the whiskey and vermouth.

2. Top with cherry cola.

3. Drop in a maraschino cherry.

DOOMSDAY CLOCK

Whiskey and ginger are two flavors that play off one another well, as the bite of ginger helps it stand up to the strong flavor of the spirit. The Doomsday Clock is a dark, boozy cocktail that lets the competing flavors of its primary ingredients stand on their own. The addition of simple syrup and bitters gives it another sweet yet spicy element, and lends a surprising depth of flavor to the drink.

BASIC INGREDIENTS:

 2 parts whiskey

 1 part ginger beer

 1 dash bitters

 1 dash simple syrup

 GLASSWARE:
Old Fashioned glass.

1. Stir the whiskey, bitters, and simple syrup together in an Old Fashioned glass.

2. Top with ginger beer.

WHISKEY PUNCH

Plenty of people make punches with vodka, gin, or even rum, but few are bold enough to make a punch with whiskey as the base ingredient. This whiskey punch recipe is a surprisingly tasty take on the idea, with orange juice and tea standing up to the flavor of the whiskey in a big way. The end result is a whiskey drink cut with citrusy freshness — a memorable harmony of flavors.

BASIC INGREDIENTS:

 2 parts whiskey

 2 parts iced tea

 1 part orange juice

 1 dash bitters

 1 orange slice (garnish)

GLASSWARE:

 Old Fashioned glass.

1. Add the liquid ingredients to a pint glass filled with ice. Stir until thoroughly mixed.

2. Strain the resulting mixture into an Old Fashioned glass (with ice if desired).

3. Add an orange slice for garnish.

This is a great drink to make in large batches. Make a party-size version and serve it in a punch bowl!

THE JUICE IS LOOSE

The Juice is Loose is similar to the Whiskey Punch cocktail in that it incorporates fruit flavors into a whiskey cocktail—a combination that many will be surprised they've never considered after tasting. The slight tartness of the cranberry complements the earthy tones of the whiskey, while the maraschino cherry garnish adds a splash of brightness to the drink's rosy glow. Elegant and delicious, The Juice Is Loose balances flavor and beauty.

BASIC INGREDIENTS:

 I part rye whiskey

 I part cranberry or grape juice

 I splash simple syrup

 I dash bitters

 I maraschino cherry (garnish)

 GLASSWARE:
Cocktail glass.

1. Add whiskey, juice, simple syrup, and bitters to a cocktail shaker filled with ice.

2. Shake well.

3. Strain the resulting mixture into a cocktail glass.

4. Garnish with a maraschino cherry.

BOURBON ICE CREAM

Some people shy away from using milk or cream in cocktails, and that's understandable. Milk has such a distinctive flavor that it's difficult to imagine it mixing well with the inherent bite of alcohol. That said, if you enjoy a White Russian (page 23) you'll want to give Bourbon Ice Cream a try. A little milk, a little vanilla, and a little sugar give this drink a delicious "melted milkshake" quality.

BASIC INGREDIENTS:

 I part bourbon whiskey

 2 parts whole milk

 I dash simple syrup

 2 or 3 drops vanilla extract

 I dash nutmeg (garnish)

 GLASSWARE:
Old Fashioned glass.

1. Add bourbon, milk, simple syrup, and vanilla extract to a cocktail shaker filled with ice and shake well.

2. Strain the resulting mixture into an Old Fashioned glass.

3. Top with a dash of nutmeg, if desired.

JAM SESSION

Whiskey doesn't get enough credit for how well it pairs with fruit liqueurs—particularly dark ones. Cherry, blackberry, and other berry liqueurs make a nice, sweet accompaniment to the often smoky, sometimes harsh bite of the whiskey. This simple rye whiskey cocktail evokes blackberry jam, resulting in the perfect drink to wind down with at the end of a long day.

BASIC INGREDIENTS:

 2 parts rye whiskey

 1 part blackberry liqueur

 1 dash simple syrup

 1 dash lemon juice

 1 lemon twist (garnish)

 GLASSWARE:
Old Fashioned glass.

1. Add whiskey, blackberry liqueur, simple syrup, and lemon juice to a cocktail shaker filled with ice.

2. Shake thoroughly.

3. Strain the resulting mixture into an Old Fashioned glass filled with ice.

4. Garnish with a twist of lemon.

A LITTLE OF THIS, A LITTLE OF THAT

What about drinks that don't fall into any particular category? You know the ones. Made with champagne, made with beer, made with vermouth, even brandy or wine. These drinks deserve our love, too.

After all, where would we be without a nice Mimosa or glass of sangria on a Saturday morning? And how are you supposed to impress your friends with your knowledge of unusual (yet elegant) cocktails without an Americano recipe?

These miscellaneous cocktails may not fit into any of the major liquor categories, but they are no less delicious for it. Chances are you'll find something that makes you wonder why you never thought of it yourself.

MIMOSA

The perfect drink for Saturday morning! How could you not love Mimosas? Sure, some people who don't like tomato juice might not like Bloody Marys. And if you're not a coffee drinker, an Irish Coffee is out. But the simple mixture of citrusy orange juice and bubbly champagne allows the Mimosa to satisfy every last individual.

BASIC INGREDIENTS

 I part orange juice

 I part champagne

 I orange slice (garnish)

 GLASSWARE:
Champagne flute.

1. Fill your champagne flute halfway with orange juice.

2. Top off with champagne. Stir if you want, or let them combine on their own. Garnish with a slice of orange.

VIRGIN MIMOSA

Mimosas are great in the morning, but sometimes you just aren't ready to start drinking that early. Perfectly understandable. Still, the bubbly lightness of a Mimosa offers enjoyment far beyond a simple buzz. In place of champagne, you can opt for a simple splash of Sprite, giving the orange juice, and your day, a little extra kick.

BASIC INGREDIENTS

 I part orange juice

 I part Sprite

 I orange slice (garnish)

GLASSWARE:
Champagne flute.

1. Fill your champagne flute halfway with orange juice.

2. Top off with Sprite and stir together.

3. Garnish with a slice of orange.

VARIATION

Sprite not your thing? Try it with ginger ale instead!

Champagne is an easy ingredient to substitute out when it comes to making virgin drinks. Its chief attribute is its fizzy sweetness, and a simple switch to Sprite, ginger ale, or even sparkling cider can turn a tasty cocktail into an equally delicious mocktail!

SANGRIA EXPRESS

1 orange (1/2 juiced, 1/2 peeled and thinly sliced)

6 oz. brandy

1 bottle red wine

4 oz. simple syrup

Turn the page for the recipe!
→

SANGRIA EXPRESS

The beauty of sangria tends to be the inclusion of as many different fruits as possible, but most of us don't have an entire fruit market at our fingertips every day. So forget sangria—go the express route and mix in a few complementary flavors for a morning beverage that's just as delicious! Makes 4-6 servings.

BASIC INGREDIENTS

 1 orange (1/2 juiced, 1/2 peeled and thinly sliced)

 6 oz. brandy

 1 bottle red wine

 4 oz. simple syrup

 **GLASSWARE:** Wine glass.

1. Juice half of the orange into a sealable container. Peel and slice the other half, and put those slices into the same container.

2. Add the brandy, red wine, and simple syrup.

3. Seal the container and refrigerate for 24 hours.

4. Pour into a pitcher or punch bowl.

DON'T FEEL LIKE WAITING? You can always skip refrigerating the sangria. The flavors won't combine quite as well (and the fruit won't soak up the flavor quite so much), but it will still be delicious! Feel free to substitute a different fruit for the orange, too.

VIRGIN SANGRIA EXPRESS

At its core, sangria is fruit juice. Much of that fruit happens to be wine, but that's okay. Virgin sangria takes that same great, grape-based flavor, and builds around it. Adding apple, orange, and lemon juice (along with some slices of fresh orange to soak up flavor), the Virgin Sangria Express is a great alternative to its boozy counterpart. Makes 4-6 servings.

BASIC INGREDIENTS

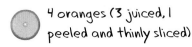
4 oranges (3 juiced, 1 peeled and thinly sliced)

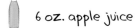
12 oz. grape juice

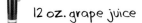
6 oz. apple juice

2 oz. lemon juice

GLASSWARE:
Wine glass.

1. Juice three oranges into a large, sealable container. Peel and slice the other orange, and put those slices into the same container.

2. Add the grape juice, apple juice, and lemon juice.

3. Seal the container and refrigerate for 24 hours.

4. Pour into a pitcher or punch bowl.

> Always feel free to add any fresh fruit you desire. Nothing tastes quite as great as fruit that's been soaking up the delicious flavors of sangria, virgin or otherwise.

AMERICANO

You might not know it, but the Americano was actually the drink originally preferred by that most famous of fictional spies, James Bond. The drink is equal parts sweet and bitter, offering a unique flavor that you might not be accustomed to. If you're willing to try something new, you can see if the American ex-pats from whom it takes its name were onto something.

BASIC INGREDIENTS

 1 oz. Campari

 1 oz. sweet vermouth

 1 oz. club soda

 1 lemon slice (garnish)

 GLASSWARE:
Old Fashioned glass.

1. Fill your glass with ice, then add the Campari and sweet vermouth. Top with club soda.

2. Garnish with a slice of lemon.

CHERRY HOOKER

Think of it as a more flavorful version of the screwdriver. The Cherry Hooker is an orange- and cherry-flavored delight, the sort of drink you might not ever think to make yourself, but once you taste it you'll wonder how you ever lived without it.

BASIC INGREDIENTS

 3 oz. cherry brandy

 Orange juice to fill

 1 dash lime juice

 1 lime wheel (garnish)

GLASSWARE:
Mason jar.

1. Add the cherry brandy to a Mason jar filled with ice, then fill the rest with orange juice.

2. Add a dash of lime juice. Stir thoroughly.

3. Garnish with a lime wheel.

SNOWBALL

Never heard of advocaat? Not surprising, since it tends to be more popular in the U.K. than the United States. Basically the European equivalent of eggnog, it's the perfect base for any winter warmer. The Snowball combines the flavors of lemonade and lime juice with a little bit of maple syrup to create a sweet-and-sour winter treat.

BASIC INGREDIENTS

 I part advocaat

 I dash lime juice

 I dash maple syrup

 I part lemonade

 I dollop whipped cream (garnish)

 I maraschino cherry (garnish)

 GLASSWARE:
Mason jar.

1. Add the advocaat and lime juice to a cocktail shaker filled with ice and shake thoroughly.

2. Strain the resulting mixture into your glass, then add maple syrup.

3. Top off the glass with lemonade and garnish with whipped cream and a maraschino cherry.

RASPBERRY FIZZ

Champagne drinks are fun, and champagne isn't used in cocktails nearly as often as it should be. Sure, you've got your Mimosas and punches, but sometimes it's nice to have a fizzy, bubbly, flavorful drink that isn't filled with a sticky, overly sweet partner. Enter the Raspberry Fizz, which pairs champagne with the flavor of delicious raspberry liqueur. Add the tartness of fresh raspberries and you've got a tasty and elegant drink you can feel good about!

BASIC INGREDIENTS:

3 parts champagne

I part raspberry liqueur

3 fresh raspberries
(garnish)

GLASSWARE:
Champagne flute.

1. Pour champagne into champagne flute.

2. Top with raspberry liqueur.

3. Drop some fresh raspberries into the drink to soak up some of the great flavor.

KOMBUCHA SANGRIA (WHITE)

If you enjoy kombucha, chances are you can imagine how well it would work in sangria. It's fizzy, it's fruity, and it's got a tiny hint of vinegar that plays perfectly against wine and fruit juice. This particular recipe is for a quick white sangria (no need to steep anything overnight). It combines several fruity touches, including apple, grape, and peach, giving it a well-rounded flavor profile that you're sure to love.

BASIC INGREDIENTS:

3 parts apple kombucha

3 parts white wine

1 part lemon seltzer

1 part white grape/ peach juice

1 handful sliced strawberries (garnish)

GLASSWARE:

Mason jar.

1. Add ice to a mason jar. Pour in the kombucha and white wine.

2. Add the seltzer and white grape/ peach juice. Avoid shaking the drink around too much, as the kombucha is extremely fizzy.

3. Float some sliced strawberries on top to pretty it up.

Try using a sparkling white wine or sparkling rosé to give your sangria an extra boost. Both go very well with kombucha!

KOMBUCHA SANGRIA (RED)

If you're more of a red sangria person, this red wine version of kombucha sangria will be right up your alley. Pinot Noir works best here, but feel free to choose any red wine you like. The simple addition of a little pomegranate kombucha and fresh pomegranate seeds really elevate this drink, giving it a lightness that makes for a perfect brunch cocktail.

BASIC INGREDIENTS:

 3 parts pomegranate Kombucha

 3 parts Pinot Noir (or your choice of red wine)

 1 part grapefruit seltzer

 1 part cranberry juice

 1 handful pomegranate seeds (garnish)

GLASSWARE:
 Mason jar.

1. Add ice to a mason jar. Pour in the kombucha and red wine.

2. Add the seltzer and cranberry juice. Avoid shaking the drink around too much as the kombucha is extremely fizzy.

3. Float some pomegranate seeds on top.

PROSECCO SOUP

Champagne soup is a popular party drink in France, but since prosecco is rapidly gaining popularity, here is a little twist on the idea. It's simple, really: a little fizz, a little fruit, a little sugar, and voila: A delicious party drink to share with your friends. Mixing the drink in a large punch bowl is the way to go, and make sure you've got lots of champagne flutes on hand to serve it in. This is a drink that works best in large batches, so invite some friends.

BASIC INGREDIENTS:

 4 parts dry prosecco

 1 part Sprite

 1 part triple sec

 1 splash simple syrup

 GLASSWARE:
Champagne flute.

1. Pour the ingredients into a punch bowl filled with ice.

2. Stir thoroughly.

3. Serve in champagne flutes.

> If Sprite is a little too sweet for your liking, feel free to use lemon or lime seltzer instead.

STOUT 'N' CIDER

Beer cocktails are few and far between, but this is one you won't want to miss out on. The smooth, roasted flavor of a stout combines well with the crisp sweetness of hard cider. The result is a beverage that will definitely have you coming back for more.

BASIC INGREDIENTS:

 I part stout beer

 I part hard cider

 GLASSWARE:
Pint glass.

1. Pour the cider into a pint glass.

2. Add the stout by pouring it over the back of an upside-down spoon. This will help it mix with the cider and prevent the drink from becoming extremely fizzy.

3. Stir together.

VIRGIN STOUT 'N' CIDER

How can you make a virgin version of a drink made entirely from alcoholic ingredients? With a little creativity, that's how. The beauty of the Virgin Stout 'N' Cider is that it flips what makes the standard Stout 'N' Cider so great on its head. Instead of a rich, dark element mixed with a sharp, fizzy light element, the virgin version contains a rich yet light element mixed with a sharp, fizzy dark element.

BASIC INGREDIENTS:

 I part ginger beer

 I part apple cider

 GLASSWARE:
Pint glass.

1. Add the ginger beer to a pint glass.

2. Pour the apple cider over the ginger beer.

BLACK VELVET

The Black Velvet is a traditional cocktail made with stout beer and champagne. Typically, the champagne is topped with a float of Guinness rather than mixing the two together, making this another sweet-yet-malty beverage that pleases the eye as well as the palate.

BASIC INGREDIENTS:

 I part champagne

 I part Guinness (or other stout beer)

 GLASSWARE:
Champagne flute.

1. Fill a champagne flute approximately halfway with champagne.

2. Float the Guinness on top of the champagne by slowly and carefully pouring it over the back of an upside-down spoon. The result should be a bright layer of champagne beneath a layer of dark, opaque beer.

HAZE FOR DAYS

New England IPAs constitute a relatively new beer style. Hoppy and unfiltered, these beers are fruitier and hazier than what many beer drinkers are used to. The flavorful nature of this style also makes it ideal for use in cocktails. Add a little triple sec to bring out the citrus elements and mix in some rum to give it a little kick.

BASIC INGREDIENTS:

 4 parts beer
(fruit-forward IPA)

 I part light rum

 I part triple sec

 I orange slice (garnish)

 GLASSWARE:
Pint glass.

1. Pour the liquid ingredients into a pint glass (add ice if desired).

2. Stir together until mixed.

3. Garnish with a slice of orange.

CLASSIC MICHELADA

Much like The Essential Bloody Mary (page 58), the michelada is a Latin American brunch drink popularized as a hangover cure. Made from beer, lime juice, and salt (among other ingredients), it's a hodgepodge of disparate flavors that come together to form something greater than the sum of its parts. Often served with the beer bottle inverted inside the drink itself, the Classic Michelada is a cool recipe that's perfect for the morning after a night on the town.

BASIC INGREDIENTS:

 I part beer (Mexican-style lager or pilsner)

 I part tomato juice

 I dash Worcestershire sauce

 I dash lime juice

 Salt (for rimming)

 I lime wedge (garnish)

GLASSWARE:
Pint glass.

1. Add the beer, tomato juice, Worcestershire sauce, and lime juice to a pint glass filled with ice.

2. Stir together until thoroughly mixed.

3. Salt the rim of a separate pint glass and add ice as desired.

4. Strain the beer and tomato juice mixture into the salt-rimmed pint glass.

5. Garnish with a lime wedge.

Like the Bloody Mary, part of the beauty of a michelada is how customizable it is. Want to add jalapeño? Go for it! Want to swap in teriyaki sauce or soy sauce? No problem. You can even experiment with different liqueurs or skip the tomato juice entirely. It's all up to you.

MEIN LEBEN

This is not a drink for the faint of heart. Frankly, no drink with Jägermeister in it is for the faint of heart. But this drink in particular will set your pulse racing with a big boost of over-caffeinated energy. Mein Leben is a drink that you may find surprisingly tasty, as both Red Bull and pineapple juice are known to mix well with the dark, licorice-flavored beverage. Jägermeister isn't just for college students anymore, and you'll find it plays very well with others.

BASIC INGREDIENTS:

 1 part Jägermeister

 2 parts Red Bull

 1 splash pineapple juice

 GLASSWARE:
Pint glass.

1. Add ice to a pint glass and pour in the Jägermeister and pineapple juice.

2. Top with Red Bull.

RED WINE SUNSET

You've probably heard of the Tequila Sunrise or the Vodka Sunrise, but how about a sunset? The Red Wine Sunset flips the typical "sunrise" convention on its head, floating a rich, dark layer of red wine atop a base of bright orange juice.

BASIC INGREDIENTS:

 4 parts orange juice

 1 part triple sec

 2 parts red wine

 1 orange slice (garnish)

 GLASSWARE:
Highball glass.

1. Add orange juice and triple sec to a highball glass filled with ice. Stir until thoroughly mixed.

2. Using the back of a spoon, carefully float the red wine on top of the orange juice mixture.

3. Garnish with an orange slice.

CIDER 75

The French 75 (page 185) is a classic champagne and gin cocktail. The Cider 75 takes that traditional recipe and gives it an apple-flavored makeover. As hard cider continues to grow in popularity, you'll find that it can be a flavorful replacement for champagne or prosecco. With a little apple brandy to take the place of gin, the Cider 75 is a fun, offbeat twist on a classic.

BASIC INGREDIENTS:

I sugar cube

I part apple brandy

2 parts dry hard cider

I lemon twist (garnish)

GLASSWARE:
Champagne flute.

1. Place a sugar cube at the bottom of a champagne flute.

2. Add the apple brandy, then the hard cider.

3. Garnish with a twist of lemon.

PUMPKIN PIE TEA LATTE

The Pumpkin Pie Tea Latte is the perfect warming beverage for a cold fall day. It combines a reviving mug of black tea with the light, airy texture of frothed milk. Add some velvety Baileys Irish Cream and a sprinkling of pumpkin pie spice and you've got a slightly boozy beverage that will keep you both warm and refreshed on the coldest of days.

BASIC INGREDIENTS:

 4 parts black tea (hot)

 1 part milk (frothed)

 1 part Baileys Irish Cream

 1 dash pumpkin pie spice

GLASSWARE:

 Mug.

1. Fill a mug about 2/3 of way with hot black tea.

2. Add Baileys Irish Cream and stir together.

3. Top with frothed milk.

4. Add a dash of pumpkin pie spice atop the frothed milk.

> Baileys has branched out beyond simple Irish cream. They now offer many different variations on their classic recipe, including flavored liqueurs and a vegan Irish cream alternative.

CHICAGO SPECIAL

Chicago is known for a lot of things: the Cubs, the wind, Michael Jordan, deep-dish pizza, and… Malört. Malört is a specialty liqueur created by the Chicago-based Carl Jeppson Company. It has become a local staple, despite the fact that the wormwood it contains gives it an extremely bitter profile. Not everyone from Chicago drinks Malört, but trying it is certainly viewed as a rite of passage, and—despite a flavor described as "grapefruit mixed with gasoline"—it can be used to make some tasty cocktails.

BASIC INGREDIENTS:

I part Malört

2 parts grapefruit juice

I orange wedge (juiced)

I orange twist (garnish)

GLASSWARE:
Cocktail glass.

1. Add the Malört and grapefruit juice to a cocktail shaker filled with ice, as well as the juice from one orange wedge. Shake vigorously.

2. Strain the resulting mixture into a cocktail glass.

3. Take an orange twist and rub it rind-side down along the rim of the cocktail glass.

4. Drop the orange twist into the bottom of the glass.

NON-ALCOHOLIC

You don't need alcohol to have a good time, and you *definitely* don't need alcohol to enjoy a delicious drink. In fact, as you might have noticed, a huge percentage of cocktails are based on trying to drown out the flavor of the alcohol rather than enhance it. With that in mind, why not just eliminate the alcohol and enjoy some delicious flavor combinations as they were meant to be?

Over the course of the book, we've sprinkled in a number of alcohol-free alternatives to both new and classic cocktails. But don't worry—we won't make you flip through the whole book to find what you're looking for. We've got everything indexed right here!

Some of these mocktails are based on existing cocktails, while others are simply fantastic drinks that stand on their own. These drinks are perfect for a night when you just want to stay in, or when you want to go out without worrying about how you'll get home. Who needs booze? Forget cocktails—give these delicious mocktails a try!

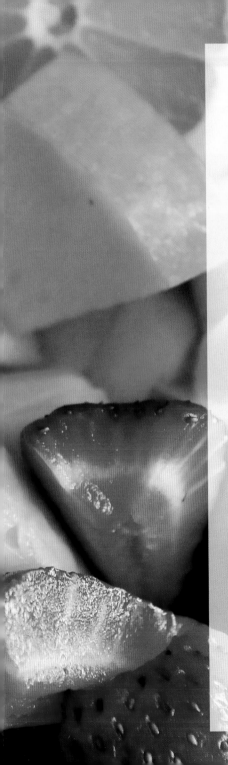

INDEX OF VIRGIN VERSIONS

CRIMSON LEMONADE

Lemonade and its dozens of variations provide a plethora of refreshing options for a hot summer day, but have you ever thought of adding a splash of grenadine? The subtle cherry or pomegranate flavor (depending on your preferred grenadine) adds a little something special to this traditional drink, and the crimson color is a beautiful departure from the norm.

BASIC INGREDIENTS

8 oz. lemonade

1 splash grenadine

GLASSWARE:

Mason jar.

1. Pour lemonade into a Mason jar filled with ice.

2. Top with a splash of grenadine.

SHIRLEY TEMPLE

Probably the most famous mocktail of all, the Shirley Temple takes a few classic secondary ingredients (grenadine and lime juice) and combines them with sweet ginger ale rather than alcohol. Perfect for both kids and adults looking to add a little extra flair to their soft drink, the Shirley Temple is as much of an attention grabber as its curly-haired namesake was.

BASIC INGREDIENTS

 12 oz. ginger ale

 1 splash grenadine

 1 dash lime juice

 1 maraschino cherry (garnish)

 GLASSWARE: Highball glass.

1. Add ice to your glass, then pour in the ginger ale.

2. Top with a splash of grenadine and a dash of lime juice. Garnish with a maraschino cherry.

ROY ROGERS

Arguably as famous as the Shirley Temple (although less adorably named), the Roy Rogers simply substitutes cola for the Shirley Temple's ginger ale. It's simple, tasty, and spices up an otherwise dull beverage. Who could say no to a little extra flavor in regular old cola?

BASIC INGREDIENTS

12 oz. cola

1 dash grenadine syrup

1 dash lime juice

1 maraschino cherry (garnish)

GLASSWARE:
Highball glass.

1. Add ice to your glass, then pour in the cola.

2. Top with a splash of grenadine and a dash of lime juice.

3. Garnish with a maraschino cherry.

VIRGIN FIZZ

If you're staying sober, it can sometimes feel like you're missing out, especially during celebrations like New Year's Eve, where toasting champagne is a tradition few can say no to. Well, don't worry: even if you can't partake of the champagne, there's no reason you can't participate in the toast. The Virgin Fizz takes the bubbly fizz of champagne and replaces it with non-alcoholic alternatives.

BASIC INGREDIENTS:

 I part ginger ale

 2 parts seltzer (any flavor)

 I raspberry (garnish)

GLASSWARE:
Champagne flute.

1. Pour the ginger ale and seltzer into a champagne flute.

2. Drop in one fresh raspberry as garnish.

DRINK RECOMMENDATIONS

Need a little help expanding your tastes? Don't worry, we've got you covered. Just think of a drink you've enjoyed, and we'll let you know which recipes in this book will scratch that same itch. Here are 18 favorites paired with a few recommendations to get you started.

If you like the Classic Old Fashioned, you might also like: Classic Manhattan, Rob Roy, Irish Rose, Mish Mash, Americano, Classic Mint Julep, Mojito Express, Negroni, Vodka Negroni.

If you like the Classic Gimlet, you might also like: French 75, Classic Gin and Tonic, Classic Martini, Blastoff, Mint Mule, Classic Cosmopolitan, Mexican Mule, Classic Mint Julep.

If you like the Mimosa, you might also like: Screwdriver, Vodka Sunrise, Tequila Sunrise.

If you like the Classic Cosmopolitan, you might also like: Classic Martini, The Dirty Spy, Cherry Lime Spike, Not-Quite Collins, Negroni, Vodka Negroni, Classic Margarita.

If you like the Mai Tai, you might also like: Your Tai, Vanilla Float, Island Punch.

If you like a daiquiri, you might also like: Daiquiri Twist, Gimlet, Margarita.

If you like the White Russian, you might also like: Quickslide, Strawberries and Cream, Creamsicle, Bourbon Ice Cream, Maple Creamer, Mexican Chocolate.

If you like the Piña Colada, you might also like: Cidermeister, Coconut Margarita, Banana Cream Pie.

If you like the Classic Martini, you might also like: The Dirty Spy, Daiquiri Twist, Classic Gimlet.

If you like the Mocha Mocha Mocha, you might also like: Quickslide, Coffee Old Fashioned, Wakeup Martini, Gin Hot Chocolate, Mexican Chocolate, Vanilla Float, Cuban Coffee, Cancun Coffee, Irish Coffee.

If you like the Sunburst, you might also like: Vodka Sunrise, Logan's Rum, Tequila Spritzer, Red Wine Sunset, Piña Colada, Gin and Juice, Tequila Sunrise.

If you like the Spiced Tea, you might also like: Peach Tree Iced Tea, Long Island Express, Classic Mint Julep, Americano, Whiskey Punch, Pumpkin Pie Tea Latte, Bourbon Sweet Tea.

If you like the Cherry Gin Sour, you might also like: Cherry Lime Spike, Classic Cosmopolitan, Caribbean Cranberry Twist, Apple Tart, Whiskey Sour, Budget Sour, Tequila Grapefruit Cocktail, Cherry Hooker.

If you like the Classic Margarita, you might also like: The Dirty Spy, Mint Mule, Classic Cosmopolitan, Pear Pressure, Piña Colada, Classic Gimlet, Shot of Marg, End of the Lime, Daiquiri Twist.

If you like the Baja Lemonade, you might also like: Mint Mule, Ring #4, Ring #5, Sunburst, Salty Mutt, Cherry Limeade Margarita, Whiskey Sour, Mimosa.

If you like the Cinnamon Apple, you might also like: Liquid Apple Pie, Peach Tree Iced Tea, Pear Pressure, Ginger Binger, Cidermeister, Tequila Cider, Stout 'N Cider, Cider 75.

If you like the Sangria Express, you might also like: Kombucha Sangria (White), Kombucha Sangria (Red), Prosecco Soup, Raspberry Fizz, Red Wine Sunset, Blueberry Sparkler, Classic Cosmopolitan, Caribbean Cranberry Twist.

TERMINOLOGY

BOURBON WHISKEY: A type of whiskey popular in the American South, distilled from a mash of at least 51% corn and aged in charred oak barrels.

COCKTAIL SHAKER: A sealed container used to mix cocktails by shaking. Usually filled with ice before use to quickly cool beverages.

DASH: A quick addition, usually of a liquid ingredient. Equal to approximately one teaspoon, but not an exact measurement.

DOLLOP: A large spoonful, usually in reference to whipped cream.

DUSTING: A small amount of a spice, usually in reference to cinnamon or nutmeg.

LIQUEUR: A sweet, flavored type of alcohol. Usually very strong in flavor and used as an accent in cocktails, rather than consumed on its own.

MIXING GLASS: A glass other than the intended drinking vessel in which to mix ingredients together.

MUDDLE: Lightly mashing ingredients in the bottom of a glass to better release their flavor. Can be done with any blunt instrument, but a specific tool known as a "muddler" also exists.

RYE WHISKEY: Similar to bourbon whiskey. Distilled from a mash of at least 51% rye and aged in charred oak barrels. Also refers to Canadian Whisky.

SCOTCH WHISKEY: A specific type of whiskey from Scotland, aged in oak casks for at least three years. The addition of peat smoke provides a smoky flavor.

SIMPLE SYRUP: Sugar water. For instructions on how to make your own, see the sidebar on page 81.

SLICE OF FRUIT: A common garnish. Refers to a slice taken from a fruit wheel.

SPLASH: A quick addition, usually of a liquid ingredient. Larger than a dash, equal to approximately one tablespoon but not an exact measurement.

STRIP: A thin slice of rind taken from a citrus fruit.

TWIST: A strip of citrus rind sliced around the diameter of the fruit to give it a corkscrew shape.

VIRGIN: Non-alcoholic.

WEDGE: A triangular slice of fruit (most commonly lime or lemon) used as a garnish. Its juice is often squeezed into the drink for added flavor.

WHEEL: A thin, circular slice of a fruit or vegetable. Most commonly used in reference to citrus fruits. Also known as "rounds."

RESOURCES

Looking for tools like cocktail shakers or mixing glasses? Look no further.

http://www.cocktailkingdom.com

http://www.beveragefactory.com

http://www.barproducts.com

For those in need of glassware, these fine retailers can provide you with everything you need.

http://www.crateandbarrel.com

http://www.pier1.com

Tired of ice melting and watering down your drink? Try some larger ice molds or whiskey stones!

http://www.whiskystones.com

http://www.thewhiskeyball.com

If you need flavored syrups for your drinks, you won't find anything better than the syrups at Torani.

https://www.torani.com

Want to learn more about cocktails? Try these fine resources for new ideas, how-tos, and educational material about all sorts of ingredients.

http://liquor.com

http://cocktails.about.com

For pitchers, punch bowls, and other party materials, check these great sites. Some even help you mix drinks right in the pitcher!

http://www.bedbathandbeyond.com

http://www.webstaurantstore.com

ABOUT THE AUTHOR

Shane Carley, a longtime aficionado of all types of alcohol, jumped at the opportunity to launch a series of cocktail books. *The Home Bartender, Second Edition* follows previous publications, including *The Martini Field Guide*, *The Mason Jar Cocktail Companion*, and *Red Cup Nation*. By day, he works as a content developer for a New Hampshire university. Weekends, however, are spent on serious book research.

INDEX

Drinks for which recipes are included in the book are italicized.

ABOUT
CIDER MILL PRESS
BOOK PUBLISHERS

Good ideas ripen with time. From seed to harvest, Cider Mill Press brings fine reading, information, and entertainment together between the covers of its creatively crafted books. Our Cider Mill bears fruit twice a year, publishing a new crop of titles each spring and fall.

Visit us online at

www.cidermillpress.com

or write to us at

12 Spring Street

PO Box 454

Kennebunkport, Maine 04046